150 Blocks for Baby Quilts

for Baby Quilts

Mix-and-match designs for cute and cozy treasures

150 Blocks **for Baby Quilts**

Mix-and-match designs for cute and cozy treasures

Susan Briscoe

C&T PUBLISHING

A QUARTO BOOK

First edition published in 2007 by
C&T Publishing Inc.
1651 Challenge Drive
Concord, CA 94520-5206
www.ctpub.com

ISBN: 978-1-57120-430-1

Conceived, designed, and produced by
Quarto Publishing plc
The Old Brewery
6 Blundell Street
London N7 9BH

QUAR: BAQ

Project editors: Anna Amari-Parker,
Rachel Mills
Editor: Miranda Smith
Art editor: Julie Joubinaux
Art director: Caroline Guest
Designer: John Thompson
Photographers: Paul Forrester,
Phil Wilkins
Illustrator: Kate Simunek

Creative director: Moira Clinch
Publisher: Paul Carslake

Repro by PICA Digital, Singapore
Printed by SNP Leefung Printers Limited,
China

Contents

Block directory
Patchwork blocks

Hidden Star Variation
1

Little Houses
2

Sailing Ship
3

Diamond
4

Dutchman's Puzzle
5

Trailing Star
6

Antique Tile
7

Jacob's Ladder
8

Off-center Log Cabin
9

Hopscotch
10

Album Block
11

Square in a Square I
12

Heart
13

Broken Dishes
14

Diagonal Four-patch Chain
15

Log Cabin with large center
16

Symmetry in Motion
17

Simplified Amish Star
18

Square Window
19

Rail Fence
20

Three-patch Quilt
21

Rolling Stone
22

Pinwheel Variation
23

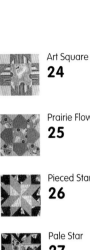

 Art Square
24

 Prairie Flowers
25

 Pieced Star Variation
26

 Pale Star
27

 Seesaw
28

 Four-patch Weave
29

 Double X
30

 Jacks on Six
31

 Counterpane
32

 Northwind
33

 Birds in Flight
34

 Cotton Reel
35

 Noah's Ark
36

 Album Star
37

 Nine Patch Fairy
38

 Abstract Flower
39

 Four Patch
40

 Yellow Star
41

 Tumbling blocks
42

 Grandmother's Flower Garden
43

 Hexagonal Flower and Pot
44

 Hexagonal Flower Duo
45

 Grandmother's Favorite Variation
46

 Maple Leaf
47

 Pinwheel
48

 Square in a Square II
49

 Antique Tile Variation
50

 Eight-point Star
51

 Beach Huts
52

Appliqué

 Curious Cat
53

 Sitting cat
54

 Cow
55

Dolphin
56

White Duck
57

Hippo
58

 Horse
59

 Lion
60

 Lioness
61

 Pig
62

 Polar Bear
63

Smiling Sun
64

Man in the Moon
65

Camel
66

Fish
67

Toadstool
68

Airplane
69

 Tiger
70

Balloon
71

 Brown Bear
72

 Cars
73

 London Bus
74

 Trucks
75

 Steam Train
76

 Tractor
77

 Chicken
78

 Dove of Peace
79

 Elephant
80

Fairy Shadow
81

Fir Tree
82

 Fox
83

 Frog
84

 Giraffe
85

 Happy Flower
86

 Lighthouse 00
87

 Little Footprints
88

 Little Handprints
89

 Overall Bill
90

 Sunbonnet Sue
91

 Rabbits
92

 Penguins
93

 Chimpanzee
94

 Whale
95

 Dalmation
96

 Rainbow Raindrops
97

 Rainbow
98

 Reindeer
99

 Rooster
100

 Seal
101

 Tree
102

 Umbrella
103

 Watering Can
104

 Zebra
105

 Yellow Duck
106

 Apple and Pear
107

 Butterflies
108

 Sheep
109

 Cloud
110

 Dancing Teddy
111

 Sitting Teddy
112

 Four-patch Heart
113

 Hearts and Leaves
114

Letters and numbers

 Alphabet "a"
115

 Alphabet "b"
116

 Alphabet "c"
117

 Alphabet "d"
118

 Alphabet "e"
119

 Alphabet "f"
120

 Alphabet "g"
121

 Alphabet "h"
122

 Alphabet "i"
123

 Alphabet "j"
124

 Alphabet "k"
125

Alphabet "l"
126

Alphabet "m"
127

Alphabet "n"
128

Alphabet "o"
129

 Alphabet "p"
130

 Alphabet "q"
131

 Alphabet "r"
132

 Alphabet "s"
133

 Alphabet "t"
134

 Alphabet "u"
135

 Alphabet "v"
136

 Alphabet "w"
137

 Alphabet "x"
138

Alphabet "y"
139

Alphabet "z"
140

Number "0"
141

Number "1"
142

Number "2"
143

Number "3"
144

Number "4"
145

Number "5"
146

Number "6"
147

Number "7"
148

Number "8"
149

Number "9"
150

Introduction

Patchwork and appliqué have long been used in quiltmaking. This book is your source and guide to creating wonderful quilts for babies and toddlers that can be used daily as baby grows up, or treasured and handed down through the family.

The arrival of an infant is a unique event, so make sure you celebrate it by making a timeless keepsake. This book has been specially designed as a resource for anyone who wants to create fabulous baby quilts. To get started, simply select the blocks that you like. With a choice of 150 patchwork and appliqué blocks, plus an infinite number of color and pattern possibilities, it has never been easier. Whether for that special new addition to your family, a friend's baby shower, or as a gift for an older infant, this book contains all the designs and technical information you will need to enjoy quilting, patchwork, and appliqué.

This cute collection of easy-to-make patchwork and appliqué blocks includes traditional favorites and brand-new designs for quilters of all abilities to mix-and-match. All the block patterns shown can be easily mixed and matched and come with a complete set of instructions. Some can be grouped together to create themed quilts, tessellated for all-over patterns, or combined in sampler quilts where every block is different.

All patchwork and fused appliqué techniques, from cutting out to completing the quilt, are clearly explained using step-by-step photography. The library of appliqué templates at the back of the book provides a rich resource of images that can be combined in different ways and used to personalize an item (with individual or combined monograms, for example). Individual touches, from fabric selection to embroidered details, are also explored and there is useful information on color and fabrics, child-friendly materials, and quilt safety guidelines.

Using the mix-and-match illustrations at the bottom of the block directory pages as a starting point for your own design layouts, combine the different blocks into the quilt's pattern and create special quilts that both babies and their moms will love!

Quilt safety

Although the words "baby quilt" may bring images to mind of an infant tucked up under a quilt in his or her crib, please do not use the item in this way. Current safety advice recommends that babies **never** be allowed to sleep under a quilt because there is increased risk of crib death in infants whose heads are accidentally covered up with bedding so they are unable to breathe properly. New mothers will be aware of this through their prenatal classes.

There are plenty of other ways a quilt can be used when babies are growing up and developing—as a clean, portable mat for changing diapers or crawling, as a bright nursery decoration or wall hanging, or as a lap quilt to protect against any little unexpected accidents or spillages!

• Use only washable materials. Rinse and starch your fabrics before you begin so they are clean and free of any manufacturer's finish. Wash the quilt once again before it is used. Some quilters use only 100% cotton batting for baby quilts, and this can be machine washed easily. Synthetic fleece rather than a cotton backing gives the quilt a very soft side.

• Make sure that all appliqué pieces are sewn securely. **Do not** add any buttons or other embellishments as an infant may accidentally swallow such small pieces.

• Once the quilt is finished, check for any pins or needles that may have been left pinned in your work by mistake.

About this book

This book is packed with everything you need to make lovely quilts, including techniques, patterns, cutting guides, and design ideas. To get started, simply choose a block from the illustrated contents. Cut out the textiles following the measurements and quantities. Use the cross references in the construction information part of each directory entry to turn to the relevant technique at the beginning of the book.

Illustrated contents (pages 4–7)
View all the blocks laid out next to each other; find some you like, and use them as the starting point for your quilt.

Getting started (pages 12–31)
This section has information on equipment and techniques, including step-by-step photographs showing how to construct different kinds of blocks in patchwork and appliqué. At the end of the section, you'll find information on how to finish your quilt, from assembling the quilt top to basic quilting and binding.

Mix and match
The "Mix and Match" illustrations show ideas for arranging the blocks in the directory in different ways. Sometimes blocks may be assembled as a mirror image or turned 90-degrees for a different effect. These computer illustrations show quilts made without sashing or borders and include possibilities for tessellation. Sizes vary from small quilts only 24 inches (61 cm) square, a good size for a lap quilt or comfort blanket, to larger sizes suitable for play mats.

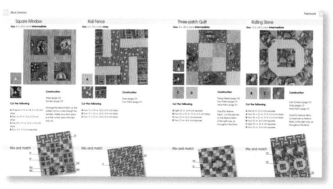

Block directory (pages 32–105)
The block directory contains all the cutting and construction information for each block, with a photograph, fabric selection, cutting instructions, construction method, and mix-and-match ideas. Imperial and metric measurements are given.

Follow either imperial or metric measurements throughout—don't switch between the two.

Appliqué templates (pages 106-123)

All appliqué templates are shown at a reduced-down percentage of the actual size (and must be enlarged on a photocopier before you begin). You will need a photocopy or tracing of the template to cut out your appliqué shape. Appliqué designs can be used as a mirror image as a feature of your quilt design. Combining two or more templates on one block or using the appliqués on larger pieces of fabric are other possibilities.

Block size

The finished size of the blocks in this book are 4 inches, 6 inches, 8 inches, and 12 inches (10.2cm, 15.2cm, 20.3cm and 30.5cm)—this means the size when they are sewn together to make the quilt top, so the actual size of the individual blocks are 4½ inches, 6½ inches, 8½ inches, and 12½ inches (11.4cm, 16.5cm, 21.6cm, and 31.8cm) wide with seam allowances. These fit together well—for example, four 6 inch (10.2cm) blocks cover the same area as one 12 inch (30.5cm) block—and allow for variety when planning your quilt. Block size can also be increased by adding a border to the block (see Borders, page 25). They also work well for small quilts just 24 inches (62.3cm) square, a good size for a toddler's comfort blanket or a small lap quilt. Use quarter-inch (6mm) seams throughout.

Planning your quilt

Once you have decided which blocks you would like to use, make a simple plan of your quilt on graph paper, using one square to represent 1 inch (2.5 cm) and writing down the number of each block in the relevant square. The mix-and-match features show various ways of combining different block sizes in one quilt. Remember, you can coordinate any group of blocks by making them from the same collection of fabrics.

Getting started

This section has information on equipment and techniques, including step-by-step photographs showing how to construct different kinds of blocks in patchwork and appliqué. At the end of the section, you'll find information on how to finish your quilt, from assembling the quilt top to basic quilting and binding.

Selecting fabrics

Your choice of fabric will make your baby quilt unique. Special quilt fabrics are made with patterns for babies and young children. The choice can be bewildering, so take mom's taste into consideration too!

Color themes vary from the brightest brights to subdued pastels and "country" color schemes. Babies are attracted to clear, bright colors, strong contrasts, and clear outlines. Their eyes focus at about 12 inches (30.5 cm) when they are newborn, but by about four months old, they can focus on near and far objects, and at eight months their vision is developed. They can see color from birth, but similar colors like red and orange are indistinguishable.

Designs like teddy bears, toys, alphabets, and cute animals are made with baby quilts in mind. You can buy coordinating fabrics from the same color range, or just use a few baby fabrics with other fabrics from your collection. Many quilt stores sell pre-cut bundles of coordinating fabrics, perfect if you don't have much time to shop. Stripes, spots, and shaded fabrics will make the quilt lively. Stripes can be used to add a sense of movement to a design. Batik fabrics have unrepeated color variations across the pattern, allowing a variety of colors to be cut from one piece of fabric. Marbled or mottled fabrics are better for large areas, like backgrounds, because permanent stains are more visible on plain fabrics.

Large scale novelty prints are good for "I-spy" quilts for toddlers. Think about including lots of different colors and shapes—the quilt can be a way of learning colors and images. Once children begin to recognize photographs, think about photo-printing

Two popular nursery themes in quilt fabrics—seashore images and bright, friendly animals.

Deep yellow accent textile continues the theme

Seashore fabric with clear motifs — livey boats buffeted by wild waves

Strongly contrasting coordinating print

Clear mid-tone fabric

Jazzy stripes in bright clear colors add movement

Cartoon-style animals are great for an "I-spy" center

Vivid marbled batik fabric gives depth and added interest

onto fabric—blocks like "Jungle Diamond" are ideal for photos. Older brothers and sisters might enjoy decorating cotton with fabric crayons for a quilt. Appliqué blocks can have colorful and interesting backgrounds too.

Fabric for patchwork should be 100% cotton, "dress weight," to allow for easy piecing and easy care. Other washable fabrics, such as towelling, soft jersey (backed with interfacing), velvet, cotton sateen, or fleece, can be used for the centers of simpler blocks like block 49 or block 32.

Bright and lively abstract prints–great for baby quilts.

Calculating fabric quantities

For an idea of how much fabric you need, note down how many blocks you want to make, then the sizes and number of pieces for each fabric. Multiply these together. For example, if you need four 2 ½ inch (6.4 cm) squares for each block and there are twenty blocks, you will need 80 squares. To cut these in four rows of twenty squares across 42 inch (105 cm) wide fabric would require 15 inches (38.1 cm) of fabric, allowing 15 squares in each row. Add a little extra in case the fabric is cut slightly off the grain and remember you cannot use the selvages! If the fabric is "fussy cut," meaning that you must select a particular motif or stripe direction, you will need more fabric. If you don't have enough of one fabric, substitute a similar tone. Try reducing the number of fabrics used in a block, changing the light/dark placement, or coordinating appliqué blocks by using the same fabrics.

Equipment

You many already have the following equipment—if not, there are plenty of quilt stores to help you out! Specialist equipment can also be bought by mail order or over the Internet (see Suppliers, page 127).

Scissors

Use fabric scissors for cutting fabric, embroidery scissors for cutting threads, and paper scissors for rough cutting paper-backed fusible webbing.

Pins and safety pins

Select fine pins, such as good quality dressmaking pins or "silk pins," for piecing patchwork. "Flower pins" have a flat head so they don't twist on the fabric. Safety pins can be used to hold the quilt layers together for quilting, instead of basting.

Needles for machine sewing

"Universal" needles, in size 10-12 (USA) or 70 or 80 (European) are good for machine sewing. "Quilting" needles are sharper and best for machine quilting. Try "Microtex" for finer fabrics and silks.

Needles for hand sewing

A selection of "sharps" is useful for basting layers before quilting. "Betweens" or smaller sharps can be used for hand quilting. A "crewel" embroidery needle is good for finishing off loose quilting threads because the longer eye is easy to thread.

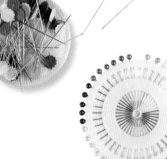

Hand-quilting threads

Hand quilting threads are treated for smooth hand sewing. Other threads can be treated with beeswax or silicone wax to resist knotting—pull the thread over the edge of the wax block several times.

All-purpose threads

Medium thickness (50s) cotton sewing thread is best for piecing. Choose a neutral color that blends with your fabrics. Thicker (30s or 40s) cotton thread can be used for machine or hand quilting. Special quilting threads include variegated thread.

Rotary cutter

A cutter with a 28mm or 45mm blade will be most useful (blades are sold in metric sizes only). Try out several cutters to find one that suits your hand best. The blades are razor sharp, so always replace the blade guard after cutting and never leave the cutter where children or pets can reach it. The cutter must be used with a mat.

Cutting mat

A large mat is best—an A2 size mat (approximately 18 x 24 inches or 46 x 61 cm) is a good size. Smaller mats make cutting difficult. Choose a mat with a printed grid, either imperial or metric, depending which measuring system you prefer.

Iron and board

An ordinary iron and board is fine for pressing blocks. Use the appropriate temperature setting and avoid steaming the blocks because this can distort the patchwork. Steam pressing finished blocks or quilt tops is fine. A small travel iron or a mini appliqué iron (like a soldering iron with a small triangular tip) is best for ironing on bias tape. A pressing mat or small ironing board is convenient to use near your sewing machine.

Ruler

Rulers are made in many different shapes and sizes. A rectangular ruler up to approximately 12 to 14 inches (30 to 35cm) long and 2 to 4½ inches (5 to 11.4cm) wide with 60-degree and 45-degree markings is fine. A square ruler is good for squaring up finished blocks. Look at the line markings and choose colors you will be able to see against your fabric. Use the same make of ruler whenever possible because measurements can vary slightly between manufacturers and between the ruler and mat, so double check!

Sewing machine

Useful features for patchwork and quilting include a good straight stitch and a "needle down" option. A quarter-inch (6mm) patchwork foot is essential for accurate patchwork. If you want to machine quilt, a walking foot (for straight lines) and a darning foot (also called an embroidery foot or quilting foot—for free motion quilting) will be necessary. A large space under the machine arm will allow for easier machine quilting.

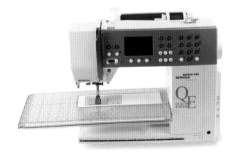

Cutting fabrics

Rotary cutting is more accurate and faster than using scissors and templates. You can cut through more than one fabric layer at a time. Make cutting easier by pressing your fabric smooth before you start. A little spray starch will keep it crisp and easy to work with.

Strips

Square off uneven ends of the fabric before you start and cut off the tightly woven selvage. Cut with the grain of the fabric (with printed stripes and checks, cut with the pattern). Turn your cutting mat 180 degrees and line up the relevant mark along the ruler—for example, 2½ inches (6.4cm) if 2 inches (5cm) is the finished strip size.

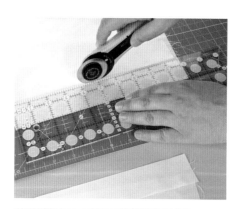

Squares and rectangles

You can cut strips to standard sizes for squares and rectangles, such as 2½ inch (6.4cm) squares and 1½ inch (3.8cm) x 2½ inch (6.4cm) rectangles very economically from the same 2½ inch (6.4cm) strip, as shown.

Triangles from squares and rectangles

Cut along one diagonal to make a half-square triangle, lining up the 45-degree angle on your ruler with the edge of the square. Cut in half again for quarter-square triangles.

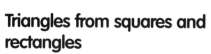

Cutting Safety

The rotary cutter has a very sharp blade and it is easy to accidentally cut yourself or others. Follow these simple rules.

- Hold the cutter in the same hand you write with at a 45-degree angle, and hold the ruler in place with your other hand.
- Cut with the blade flat against the side of your ruler—on the right if you are right-handed and on the left if you are left-handed. The patchwork piece you are cutting is under the rule.
- Use a sharp blade that is free from nicks and other damage—a dull blade requires more pressure when you cut and you risk that the blade will slip.
- Stand up to cut if you can and place the mat on a firm surface—a kitchen counter or sturdy table is ideal.
- Always cut away from yourself.
- Always replace the safety guard on the cutter—make a habit of doing this after every cut.
- Wear something on your feet when you cut, in case you drop the cutter.
- Keep cutting equipment away from children and pets.

Machine-piecing techniques

Machine-sewn patchwork is relatively quick to do. Even the most complex large block in this book is easy to make, using various simple patchwork units to build the block. To help you understand the stitching, contrasting threads have been used for the samples. Before you begin, shorten the length of the machine stitch to around two-thirds the normal length—to around 12 to 14 stitches per inch (about 1.7 to 2mm long). Use a quarter-inch (6mm) seam allowance throughout.

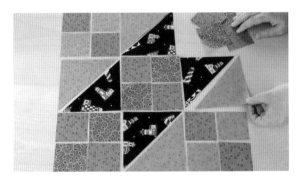

Laying out the block

Lay out the pieces before you begin sewing and join them together following the individual block instructions. Many blocks require that pieces are first sewn together in rows. The photo shows block 8. You can see it is made from five Four Patch blocks and four Half-square Triangles, sewn together as a Nine Patch.

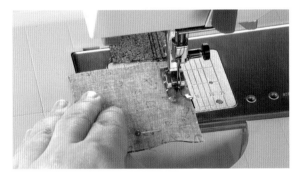

Machine piecing

Place your first two pieces right sides together, making sure the edges to be sewn line up. Use the quarter-inch (6mm) foot and line up the fabric edge with the edge of the foot when you sew (left). It may help if you sit slightly to the right of the machine needle so you can see this easily. Use a fabric scrap as a "leader" so the first patchwork stitches don't get chewed up. Longer pieces will need to be pinned—always pin at right angles to the stitching line and remove pins as you sew. Hitting a pin as you sew will break off the tip of the machine needle.

Chain piecing

Chain piecing speeds up sewing patchwork. When you have sewn your first two pieces together, don't cut the thread. Place the next two pieces together and sew them a stitch or two after the first two pieces. Continue like this to make a "chain" which can be cut up afterward (left).

Pressing patchwork

Press each stage of your patchwork as you go along. Press the seam allowance to one side because this will help stop the wadding (batting) from "bearding" or coming through the seam later. Press toward the darker fabric out of preference because pressing dark toward light can cause a shadow effect on paler fabrics. Pressing in alternate directions makes the seams interlock neatly, as shown. For blocks pieced from the center outward, such as block 9 and block 16, press seams toward the outside of the block. Press with a dry iron or just a little steam using an up and down action so the patchwork is not stretched and distorted—you are pressing, not ironing! Good pressing can really make a difference to your patchwork so get it right before you continue piecing.

Press outward from the center block on the reverse of the fabric.

Tips for patchwork

• When sewing large pieces, keep the bulk of the fabric to the left of the needle, where possible.

• Machine needles can soon become blunt. Change to a new needle after one or two projects.

• Do not sew over pins.

• If the needle breaks when stitching, try a larger needle.

• If the fabric puckers or stitches are skipped, try a smaller needle.

• Keep small scissors tied to your machine with a length of narrow ribbon so they will always be within easy reach. Trim thread tails after each seam to prevent catching them in the next seam.

Quilter's tip

Replace the standard zigzag throat plate on your machine with a straight stitch plate for patchwork, quilting, and straight stitch edging on appliqué. The needle cannot be accidentally dragged sideways, which gives a better straight stitch. Consult your machine dealer for more information. Remember to replace the zigzag plate for all but straight stitching!

Four Patch

Four Patch is one of the easiest patchwork blocks to stitch. Many blocks use a Four-patch construction, although the individual squares are also made up of patchwork, others include smaller Four-patch elements in their design.

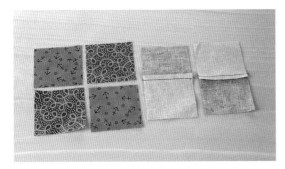

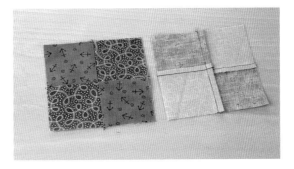

1. Arrange pairs of squares as shown, place right sides together, and sew. Press seams in opposite directions. Place the two patchwork pieces right sides together—it will be possible to butt the previous seams together neatly because the seam allowances lie on opposite sides of the seams.

2. Sew and press seams to one side. The seam allowances will line up perfectly!

Nine Patch

Arrange the pieces, sew into strips of three patches, and press seams to one side. Pressing all seams toward the darker fabric is best.

Assemble the rest of the block, following the step 2 instructions for Four Patch, above.

Like Four Patch, many blocks are made using the Nine-Patch sequence.

Block 38

Simple blocks like Nine Patch are effective for combining novelty prints with plainer designs.

Seminole Strips

To make blocks like block 40 quickly, machine sew long strips of fabric together, press and cut segments. For example, if individual squares are 2½ inches (5 cm), cut long strips 2½ inches (5 cm) wide, sew together, and cut 2½ inch (5 cm) segments. This method can be used to create parts of blocks, such as the corners of block 8. It can only be machine sewn because the first seams are cut through and hand sewing would come undone.

Half-square Triangles

This accurate method of making Half-Square Triangles avoids the necessity of sewing two bias cut edges together because the cut is made after the diagonal lines are sewn. Start by adding an extra ⅜ inch (1 cm) seam allowance to the desired finished size of your square—for example, for a 4½ inch (11.4 cm) square, cut a 4⅞ inch (12.4 cm) square. This extra allowance is already included in the cutting lists for the relevant blocks. If you would rather cut the triangles first, cut along the diagonal line before pinning and sewing.

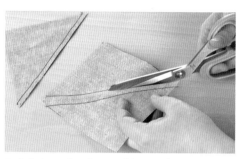

1. Draw a diagonal line on the lighter square and place squares together. Treat this line as the fabric edge, lining it up with the edge of the quarter-inch (6mm) foot, and machine sew. Sew again along the other side of the drawn line. If you have already cut the triangle, pin two triangles carefully before sewing the seam.

2. Cut along the diagonal line and press toward the darker fabric. This makes two Half-square Triangles.

3. Clip off the "dog ears" (the little points sticking out at the corners); see detail.

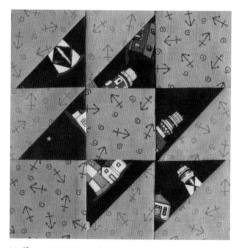

Half-square Triangles are used for blocks like this one.

Fast Corners

Here is a neat method for easily
adding triangles to the corners of a
square, by cutting out squares the
same size as the finished corners,
for example, 1½ inch (3.8 cm).

Bonus Half-square Triangle

diagonal line

anchor line

excess fabric

1. Draw a diagonal line on each square. Place
one square on the corner as shown, and sew
along the drawn line. Fold over the triangle you
have made and press. Draw and sew a parallel
line ½ inch (1.3 cm) further into the corner if you
like, to make a bonus Half-square Triangle. Use
scissors to cut between the lines on each corner.

2. Larger corner squares are used
to create a diamond in a square
(above)—here the corner squares
equal half the finished block size,
2 inches (5 cm) plus ½ inch (1.3 cm).

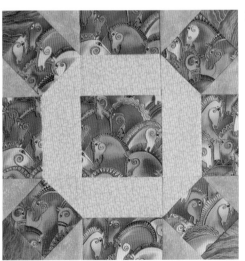

Block 22

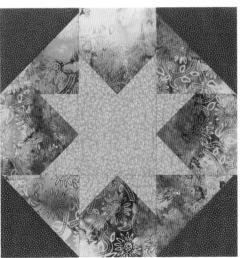

Block 1

Two blocks made with
Nine-Patch layouts—
block 22 has corner
squares made with Fast
Corners, while block 1
uses Fast Corners for the
star points.

Flying Geese and Parallelograms

Flying Geese can be made using a similar method to Fast Corners (see page 23). All Flying Geese used in this book are the same size—the rectangle is 4½ x 2½ inches (11.4 x 6.4 cm) and the squares are 2½ inches (6.4 cm). Depending on where the second triangle is positioned, a Parallelogram rather than Flying Geese can be made, as shown on the right of each photograph.

Flying Geese are used to piece various blocks, including block 2. The parallelogram is used in block 17 to give movement. The rectangle with just one triangle added is used for the star effect in block 27.

1. Cut two squares for each rectangle. Draw a diagonal line on each square. Place one square on the rectangle and sew along the drawn line. Fold over the triangle you have made, and press. Use scissors to trim away the excess fabric underneath.

Block 2

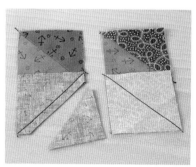

2. Repeat with the second triangle.

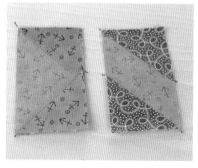

3. The finished pieces can be used in a range of blocks.

Block 17

Block 27

Log Cabin

Log Cabin blocks, like block 16, have strips sewn around a center square. Traditional centers are quite small, but for a baby quilt, you can use a pictorial fabric to effectively enlarge the center.

1. Start by pinning the ends of the strip and then add more pins along the strip. Pinning is necessary to make sure the ends of each strip line up with the block. Sew the strip. Press the seams toward the outside of the block.

2. Pin and sew the second strip. Continue adding strips in this way until the block is complete.

3. The Log Cabin light and dark effect is created by sewing the strips in pairs around the block.

Strips

Pin blocks with long strips or borders, like block 20, as you do for Log Cabin. Sew blocks of strips and then arrange them to make the block.

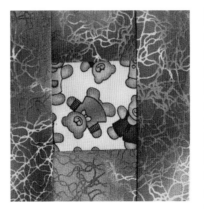

Borders

Add borders to blocks in the same way you sew the outer sections of Log Cabin. Some blocks have borders as part of their design, like blocks 12 and 19. Other blocks can be made larger by adding borders, for example to make a 6 inch (15.2cm) block fit among a group of 8 inch (20 cm) blocks.

English paper piecing: hexagons

Sewing hexagons, diamonds, triangles, and other mitered shapes together is easier with English paper piecing. Blocks using English paper piecing to create appliqué motifs include block 43 Grandmother's Flower Garden and block 44 Hexagonal Flower and Pot.

 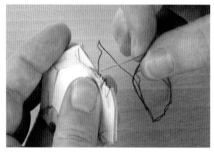 

1. Cut the paper templates to the exact finished size of each piece and baste the fabric patches around them, sewing through the paper.

2. Right sides together, oversew or whipstitch the pieces together, starting and finishing the sewing with a knot, about ¼ inch (6mm) from the corner of the patch.

3. Press the patchwork when complete and remove the papers.

English paper piecing: diamonds

Oversew diamonds into groups of three, as shown for block 42. The fabric allowances will form points beyond the ends of the diamonds. These can be tucked in when the piece is appliquéd.

Appliqué

Appliqué involves laying and stitching one piece of fabric over another to create a decorative design. It is excellent for pictorial designs, such as animals and objects. Fused or bonded appliqué is easy to do. Check the details of each appliqué design before you begin and note where appliqué pieces overlap. Appliqué templates can be sewn as mirror images. Several templates can be combined on a larger block or appliquéd to a long border or larger quilt center.

Fusible bias appliqué

Ready made fusible bias strips are easy to use and can represent details like flower stems. This is a Japanese product but is available in quilt stores. They are easier to apply if you use a mini iron or a travel iron.

Following the manufacturer's instructions, simply iron strips on and hand sew in place with small stitches, coming up through the very edge of the tape and down through the backing fabric. Tuck the ends under other appliqué edges.

Machine appliqué

English paper pieced flowers and blocks are appliquéd by machine without any need for bonding. Press the patchwork and remove papers. Pin the patchwork to the background fabric. Machine sew around the edge, making sure the seam allowances remain turned under. Machine blanket stitch is effective.

Fused appliqué

There are several brands and weights of fusible web. Some make a temporary bond, holding the appliqué in place until it is secured by stitching, while others have a very strong bond but make the fabric rigid and difficult to sew. All of them enable you to iron on ordinary fabric. Select one that has a medium bond. Check the instructions regarding ironing temperature when you buy the bonding material.

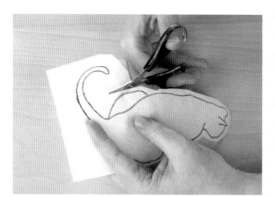

1. Make easy appliqué by ironing a fusible web backing to your fabric, cutting out the pieces, and ironing them onto a backing fabric. Begin by tracing the pattern pieces onto the paper backing, remembering to draw a mirror image of the pattern. Roughly cut around the piece.

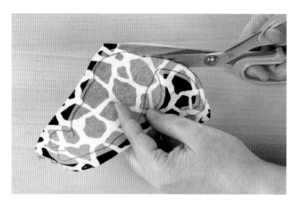

2. Following the manufacturer's instructions, iron the web onto the back of your fabric. When the piece has cooled, carefully cut around the appliqué shape. Transfer any detail lines onto the fabric by tracing against a lightbox, a backlit window, or something similar.

3. Machine sew around the appliqué several times with straight stitches for a lively but secure finish. Add details such as whiskers, eyes, feathers, and so on.

Three or four parallel lines of running stitch allow for plenty of detail and give a sharp, strong edge. It doesn't matter if the stitch lines cross.

Try different stitches to edge your appliqué. Satin stitch (machine zigzag with a short stitch length) gives a more solid edge.

Machine blanket stitch gives blocks a folk art look. Select a thread color that will make the appliqué stand out from the background. Variegated threads make the outline appear softer.

Completing the quilt

The quilt batting is sandwiched between the backing and the quilt top and is quilted by hand or machine.

Borders and sashing

Blocks can be sewn together into strips, pressed, and the strips sewn to each other to make a quilt top. As you do with sewing blocks, press these seams in opposite directions. If combining patchwork blocks with appliqué blocks, it is easier to press toward the appliqué because these do not have seams at the outer edges.

Pin blocks carefully and join them neatly.

You may wish to add borders or sashing to each block. Borders are strips added to blocks individually, while sashing is a strip sewn between adjacent blocks. An outer border can be added in the same way, taking measurements through the center of the quilt top rather than along the edge. For borders, the first two borders will be as long as the side of the block. The next two borders are longer, equalling the block plus the finished width of the first two borders. If some blocks are slightly smaller or larger than you expected, add borders and trim so all the blocks are the same size. Pin border strips in place before sewing.

A 6 inch (15cm) block is turned into an 8 inch (20cm) block by adding a 1 inch (2.5cm) border.

Use the edge of a teaspoon to flick up the point of the needle when basting—it saves sore fingers.

Sandwiching with fleece

Fleece has become very popular as a quilt backing for children's quilts. You will still need three layers. The fleece is the bottom layer. The middle layer should be plain calico or a similar plain, light cotton fabric. The quilt top goes on top.

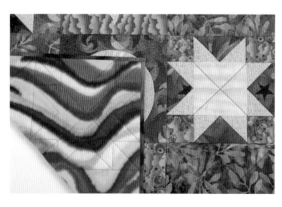

A brightly colored, highly patterned fleece backing makes a cozy play mat.

Sandwiching the top, batting, and backing

If you need to join fabric for the quilt backing, use two vertical seams rather than one seam down the center of the quilt back where the quilt may be repeatedly folded during its lifetime. The backing and batting should be about 2 inches (5cm) larger than the quilt top all around. Press the fabrics.

Smooth out the backing on a flat, clean surface, covering any important table tops with heavy cardboard or plywood. Hold the edges down with masking tape placed at close intervals. Spread the wadding on top and smooth out. Lay the quilt top over the wadding and smooth out, making sure block corners are square. Starting at the center, baste the layers together.

Quilting by hand

1. To hand quilt, start by tying two knots at the end of the quilting thread. From the front of the quilt, take a long stitch in the opposite direction to the way you will quilt and literally "pop" the two knots through the fabric and into the wadding. With your left hand under the quilt, take small running stitches in a rocking motion, going through all the layers. Feel the needle point emerging under the quilt with your left hand and immediately push the point up again.

2. Take several stitches at a time before pulling the thread through. At the end, turn the quilt over, tie two more knots, and pop these through the backing and into the quilt.

Two rows of hand stitching are used to outline the square at the center of this block.

Machine quilting

Machine quilting can start and finish at the edge of the quilt to avoid lots of loose thread ends that you would have to sew in afterward. Continuous line patterns are easiest to quilt. Choose toning threads a shade darker than the background fabrics, unless you want a contrast. The samples use red thread for clarity.

A walking foot feeds the quilt top and backing through at the same rate, preventing unsightly puckering. It is good for quilting straight lines "in the ditch" (the seam line), parallel lines, grids, and gentle curves.

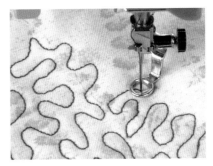

Free-motion quilting is done with the machine feed dogs set down.

Binding and finishing

A simple single-strip binding finishes off the quilt neatly. Trim the backing and batting to match the edge of the quilt top. Tack or sew all around the top, close to the edge, to hold the layers together while binding. Decide if you want to bind the top and bottom first or the sides first.

1. Cut binding strips on the straight grain for wall hangings. Cut 1½ inch (3.8mm) binding strips. The first two strips will be the same length as the edge to be bound and the second two will be 2 inches (5cm) longer than the remaining edges.

2. Pin the first two strips to the corresponding quilt edges along the front of the quilt, setting the strip edge approximately ¼ inch (6mm) away from the quilt edge, and sew.

3. Fold the binding around the edge, turn under a ¼ inch (6mm) allowance, and hem by hand with small stitches to the back of the quilt. Repeat for the two remaining edges, but allow the binding to overlap by 1 inch (2.5cm) at each end when machine sewing. Fold and sew in these ends before hemming the binding to the back.

Finish off the quilt edge with a single strip binding.

section two
Block directory

The block directory contains all the cutting and construction information for each block, with a photograph, fabric selection, cutting instructions, construction method, at-a-glance symbols and ideas for mixing-and-matching blocks together to make a quilt. Imperial and metric measurements are given. Follow either imperial or metric measurements throughout—don't switch between the two.

Patchwork

The patchwork blocks can be mixed and matched on their own or with the appliqué blocks from the next section (see page 62). Every block has a mix-and-match idea, or try your own arrangements. You can combine the blocks you like by coordinating your fabrics.

Hidden Star Variation

Size: 12 in. (30.5cm) • **intermediate**

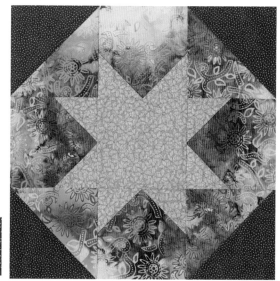

Cut the following

A Two 4⅞ in. (12.4cm) squares
B Two 4⅞ in. (12.4cm) squares
B Four 4½ in. (11.4cm) squares
C One 4½ in. (11.4cm) square
C Eight 2½ in. (6.4cm) squares

Construction

Half-square Triangles (page 22)
Fast Corners (page 23)
Nine Patch (page 21)

Mix and match

4

1

Little Houses

Size: 12 in. (30.5 cm) • **advanced**

Sailing Ship

Size: 12 in. (30.5 cm) • **advanced**

Cut the following

A Four 2½ in. (6.4 cm) squares
B One 4½ x 2½ in. (11.4 x 6.4 cm) strip
C Two 4½ x 2½ in. (11.4 x 6.4 cm) strips
D One 4½ x 2 ½ in. (11.4 x 6.4 cm) strip
D Two 2½ in. (6.4 cm) squares
E One 4½ x 2½ in. (11.4 x 6.4 cm) strip
E Two 2½ in. (6.4 cm) squares
F Two 4½ x 2½ in. (11.4 x 6.4 cm) strips
G One 4½ x 2½ in. (11.4 x 6.4 cm) strip
H Two 8½ x 2½ in. (21.6 x 6.4 cm) strips
H Two 12½ x 2½ in. (30.5 x 6.4 cm) strips

Construction

Flying Geese (page 24)
Strips (page 25)
Borders (page 25)

Cut the following

A One 8½ x 2½ in. (21.6 x 6.4 cm) strip
A One 6½ x 2½ in. (16.5 x 6.4 cm) strip
A Two 4½ x 2½ in. (11.4 x 6.4 cm) strips
A Three 2⅞ in. (7.3 cm) squares
B One 8½ x 2½ in. (21.6 x 6.4 cm) strip
B Two 2½ in. (6.4 cm) squares
C One 8½ x 2½ in. (21.6 x 6.4 cm) strip
D Four 2½ in. (6.4 cm) squares
D Three 2⅞ in. (7.3 cm) squares
E Two 12½ x 2½ in. (30.5 x 6.4 cm) strips

Construction

Half-square Triangles
(page 22)
Flying Geese
(page 24)
Borders (page 25)

Sew fabric D so the stripes
run horizontally on the
ship's sails.

Mix and match

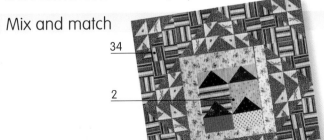

34

2

Mix and match

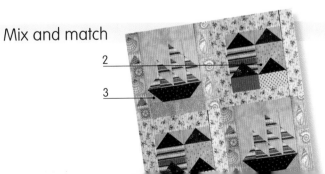

2

3

Jungle Diamond

Size: 6 in. (15.2cm) • **easy**

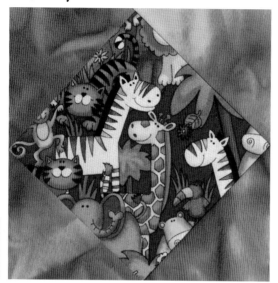

Cut the following

A One 6½ in. (16.5cm) square
B Four 3½ in. (8.9cm) squares

Construction

Fast Corners (page 23)

Use a feature fabric for A.

Dutchman's Puzzle

Size: 8 in. (20.3cm) • **intermediate**

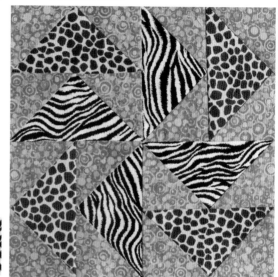

Cut the following

A Four 4½ x 2½ in. (11.4 x 6.4cm) strips
B Four 4½ x 2½ in. (11.4 x 6.4cm) strips
C Sixteen 2½ in. (6.4cm) squares

Construction

Half-square Triangles
(page 22)
Strips (page 25)
Four Patch (page 21)

Cut striped fabrics so the
stripes run the same way
on each patch.

Mix and match

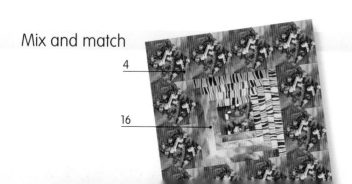

4

16

Mix and match

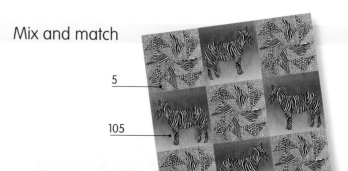

5

105

Trailing Star

Size: 8 in. (20.3 cm) • **intermediate**

A

B

C

Cut the following

A Sixteen 2½ in. (6.4 cm) squares
B Four 4½ x 2½ in. (11.4 x 6.4 cm) strips
C Four 4½ x 2½ in. (11.4 x 6.4 cm) strips

Construction

Flying Geese (page 24)
Strips (page 25)
Four Patch (page 21)

Cut striped fabrics so the stripes run the same way on each patch.

Antique Tile: Stripes and Spots

Size: 6 in. (15.2 cm) • **easy**

A

B

C

Cut the following

A One 2½ in. (6.4 cm) square
A Four 1½ in. (3.8 cm) squares
A Four 1½ x 2½ in. (3.8 x 6.4 cm) strips
B Four 1½ in. (3.8 cm) squares
B Four 1½ x 2½ in. (3.8 x 6.4 cm) strips
C Four 1½ x 2½ in. (3.8 x 6.4 cm) strips

Construction

Strips (page 25)
Nine patch (page 21)

Cut striped fabrics so the stripes run the same way on each patch.

Mix and match

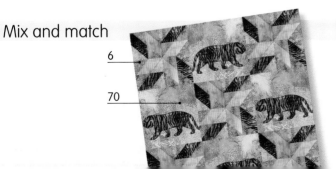

6

70

Mix and match

105

58

61

60

94

7

66

Jacob's Ladder

Size: 12 in. (30.5 cm) • **intermediate**

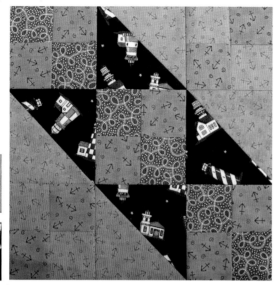

Cut the following

A Ten 2½ in. (6.4 cm) squares
B Two 4⅞ in. (12.4 cm) squares
C Six 2½ in. (6.4 cm) squares
D Four 2½ in. (6.4 cm) squares
D Two 4⅞ in. (12.4 cm) squares

Construction

Four Patch (page 21)
Half-square Triangles (page 22)
Nine Patch (page 21)

The two-fabric variation of this block
is known as Railroad.

Off-center Log Cabin

Size: 12 in. (30.5 cm) • **intermediate**

Cut the following

A One 1½ in. (3.8 cm) wide strip in
each of the following lengths—2½,
3½, 5½, 6½, 8½, 11½, 12½ in. (6.4,
8.9, 16.5, 21.6, 24, 29.2, 31.8 cm)
B One 2½ in. (6.4 cm) square
B One 2½ in. (6.4 cm) wide strip
in each of the following lengths—
3½, 5½, 6½, 8½, 9½, 11½ in. (8.9,
14, 16.5, 21.6, 24, 29.2 cm)

Construction

Log Cabin (page 25)

Swap the position of light and
dark strips in this block to
create complex curves.

Mix and match

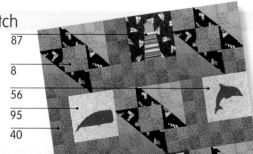

87
8
56
95
40

Mix and match

9

Hopscotch

Size: 8 in. (20.3 cm) • **intermediate**

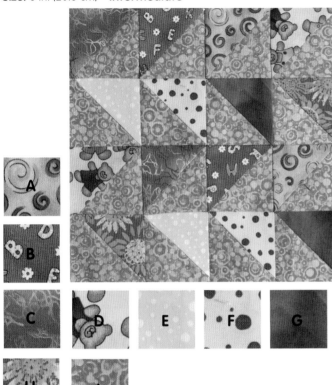

Cut the following

A–H One 2⅞ in. (7.3 cm) square of each fabric
I Eight 2⅞ in. (7.3 cm) squares

Construction

Half-square Triangles (page 22)
Strips (page 25)

Album Block

Size: 12 in. (30.5 cm) • **intermediate**

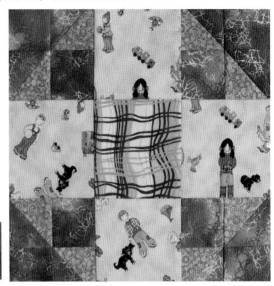

Cut the following

A Eight 2½ in. (6.4 cm) squares
A Four 2⅞ in. (7.3 cm) squares
B Four 2⅞ in. (7.3 cm) squares
C Four 4½ in. (11.4 cm) squares
D One 4½ in. (11.4 cm) square

Construction

Half-square Triangles (page 22)
Four Patch (page 21)
Nine Patch (page 21)

Mix and match

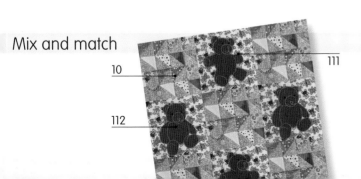

10
111
112

Mix and match

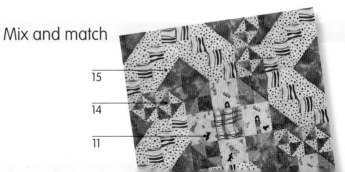

15
14
11

Square in a Square I

Size: 4 in. (10.2 cm) • **easy**

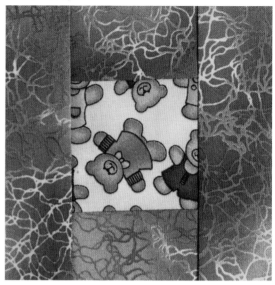

Construction

Borders (page 25)

Cut the following

A One 2½ in. (6.4 cm) square
B Two 1½ x 2½ in. (3.8 x 6.4 cm) strips
B Two 1½ x 4½ in. (3.8 x 11.4 cm) strips

Mix and match

14
12
11
11

Heart

Size: 8 in. (20.3 cm) • **intermediate**

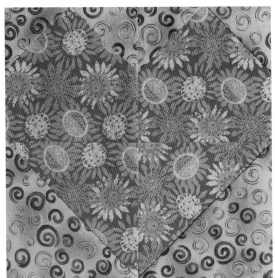

Cut the following

A One 4⅞ in. (12.4 cm) square
A Two 4½ in. (11.4 cm) squares
B One 4⅞ in. (12.4 cm) square
B Four 2½ in. (6.4 cm) squares

Construction

Four Patch (page 21)
Half-square Triangles
(page 22)
Fast Corners (page 23)
Flying Geese (page 24)

Broken Dishes

Size: 4 in. (10.2 cm) • **intermediate**

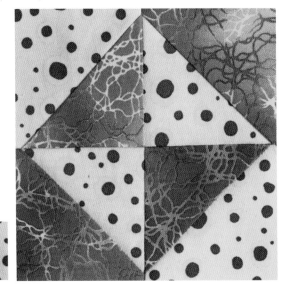

Cut the following

A Two 2⅞ in. (7.3 cm) squares
B Two 2⅞ in. (7.3 cm) squares

Construction

Half-square Triangles (page 22)
Four Patch (page 21)

Mix and match

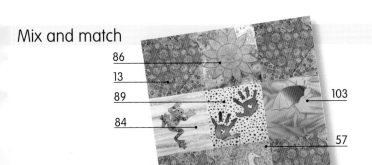

86
13
89
84
103
57

Mix and match

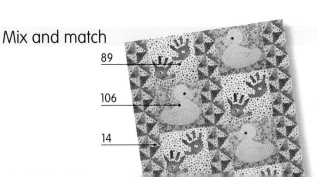

89
106
14

Diagonal Four-patch Chain

Size: 8 in. (20.3 cm) • *intermediate*

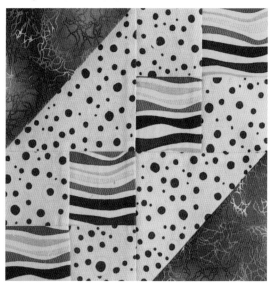

Construction

Half-square Triangles (page 22)
Four Patch (page 21)

Cut the following

A Four 2½ in. (6.4 cm) squares
B Four 2½ in. (6.4 cm) squares
B One 4⅞ in. (12.4 cm) square
C One 4⅞ in. (12.4 cm) square

Log Cabin with Large Center

Size: 12 in. (30.5 cm) • *intermediate*

Construction

Log Cabin (page 25)

Use a feature fabric for the large center square.

Cut the following

A One 4½ in. (11.4 cm) square
B One 1½ in. (3.8 cm) strip—
4½, 5½, 6½, 7½, 8½, 9½, 10½, 11½ in. (11.4, 14, 16.5, 19, 21.6, 24, 26.7, 29.2 cm) long
C One 1½ in. (3.8 cm) strip—
5½, 6½, 7½, 8½, 9½, 10½, 11½, 12½ in. (14, 16.5, 19, 21.6, 24, 26.7, 29.2, 31.8 cm) long

Mix and match

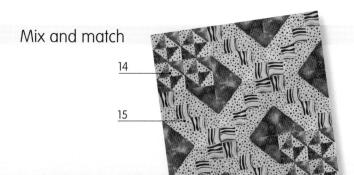

14

15

Mix and match

16

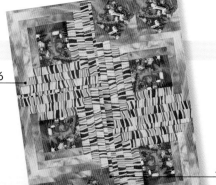

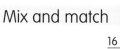

4

Symmetry in Motion

Size: 8 in. (20.3 cm) • **intermediate**

Construction

Flying Geese (page 24)
Nine Patch (page 21)

Cut the following

A One 4½ in. (11.4 cm) square
A Four 2½ in. (6.4 cm) squares
A Four 2⅞ in. (7.3 cm) squares
B Four 4½ x 2½ in. (11.4 x 6.4 cm) strips
B Four 2½ in. (6.4 cm) squares
C Four 2½ in. (6.4 cm) squares
C Four 2⅞ in. (7.3 cm) squares

Simplified Amish Star

Size: 12 in. (30.5 cm) • **intermediate**

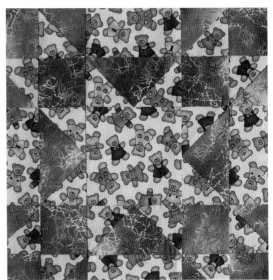

Construction

Half-square Triangles
(page 22)
Four Patch (page 21)
Flying Geese (page 24)
Strips (page 25)
Nine Patch (page 21)

Cut the following

A One 4½ in. (11.4 cm) square
A Four 4½ x 2½ in.
(11.4 x 6.4 cm) strips
A Four 2⅞ in. (7.3 cm) squares
A Eight 2½ in. (6.4 cm) squares
B Eight 2½ in. (6.4 cm) squares
B Four 2⅞ in. (7.3 cm) squares
B Four 4½ x 2½ in.
(11.4 x 6.4 cm) strips

Mix and match

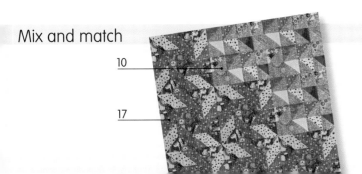

10

17

Mix and match

18

112

49

111

12

Square Window

Size: 8 in. (20.3 cm) • **intermediate**

Cut the following

A Three 6½ x 1½ in. (16.5 x 3.8 cm) strips
A Two 3 x 1½ in. (7.6 x 3.8 cm) strips
A Two 8½ x 1½ in. (21.6 x 3.8 cm) strips
B Four 3 in. (7.6 cm) squares

Construction

Strips (page 25)
Borders (page 25)

Arrange the feature fabric so the pattern forms a view though the window. Make sure each piece is in the correct place the right way up.

Rail Fence

Size: 6 in. (15.2 cm) • **easy**

Cut the following

A Four 1½ x 3½ in. (3.8 x 8.9 cm) strips
B Four 1½ x 3½ in. (3.8 x 8.9 cm) strips
C Four 1½ x 3½ in. (3.8 x 8.9 cm) strips

Construction

Strips (page 25)
Four Patch (page 21)

Mix and match

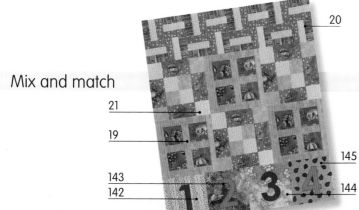

20
21
19
143
142
1 2 3
145
144

Mix and match

20
4

Three-patch Quilt

Size: 8 in. (20.3 cm) • **intermediate**

A

B

C

D

Cut the following

A Eight 2½ in. (6.4 cm) squares
B Four 4½ x 2½ in. (11.4 x 6.4 cm) strips
C Four 2½ in. (6.4 cm) squares
D Four 2½ in. (6.4 cm) squares

Construction

Flying Geese (page 24)
Four Patch (page 21)
Nine Patch (page 21)

Good for feature
fabric. Cut the patches
so the feature fabric
is the right way up
throughout the block.

Rolling Stone

Size: 12 in. (30.5 cm) • **intermediate**

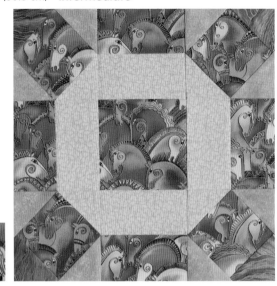

A

B

C

D

Cut the following

A Five 4½ in. (11.4 cm) squares
A Four 4½ x 2½ in. (11.4 x 6.4 cm) strips
B Four 4½ x 2½ in. (11.4 x 6.4 cm) strips
B Four 2½ in. (6.4 cm) squares
C Eight 2½ in. (6.4 cm) squares
D Four 2½ in. (6.4 cm) squares

Construction

Fast Corners (page 23)
Strips (page 25)
Nine Patch (page 21)

Good for feature fabric.
Cut patches so feature
fabric is the right way up
throughout the block.

Mix and match

110

21

Mix and match

23

22

20

Pinwheel Variation

Size: 8 in. (20.3 cm) • **intermediate**

A

B

C   D

Cut the following

A Four 4½ x 2½ in. (11.4 x 6.4 cm) strips
A Four 2½ in. (6.4 cm) squares
B Two 2½ in. (6.4 cm) squares
C Two 2½ in. (6.4 cm) squares
D Four 4½ x 2½ in. (11.4 x 6.4 cm) strips

Construction

Flying Geese (page 24)
Strips (page 25)
Four Patch (page 21)

Art Square

Size: 8 in. (20.3 cm) • **intermediate**

A

B

C   D

Cut the following

A Four 2½ in. (6.4 cm) squares
B Four 4½ x 2½ in. (11.4 x 6.4 cm) strips
C Eight 2½ in. (6.4 cm) squares
D One 4½ in. (11.4 cm) square

Construction

Flying Geese (page 24)
Nine Patch (page 21)

Feature fabric is ideal for
the center.

Mix and match

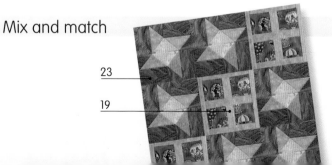

23

19

Mix and match

37

24

Prairie Flowers

Size: 12 in. (30.5 cm) • **intermediate**

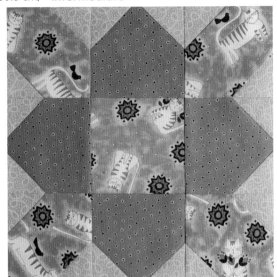

Cut the following

A Five 4½ in. (11.4 cm) squares
B Sixteen 2½ in. (6.4 cm) squares
C Four 4½ in. (11.4 cm) squares

Construction

Fast Corners (page 23)
Nine Patch (page 21)

Ideal for feature fabric.
Cut patches so the feature
fabric is the right way up
throughout the block.

Pieced Star Variation

Size: 8 in. (20.3 cm) • **intermediate**

Cut the following

A Eight 2½ in. (6.4 cm) squares
B Four 4½ x 2½ in. (11.4 x 6.4 cm) strips
B Two 2⅞ in. (7.3 cm) squares
C Four 2½ in. (6.4 cm) squares

Construction

Half-square Triangles (page 22)
Parallelograms (page 24)
Four Patch (page 21)

Mix and match

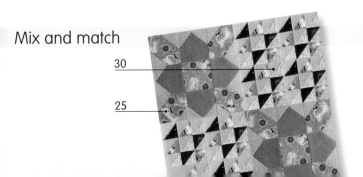

30

25

Mix and match

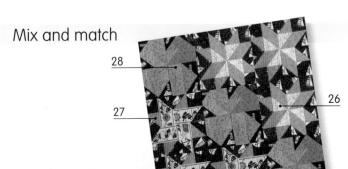

28

27

26

Pale Star

Size: 8 in. (20.3 cm) • **intermediate**

A

B

C

Cut the following

A Eight 2½ in. (21.6 cm) squares
B Four 4½ x 2½ in. (11.4 x 6.4 cm) strips
C Two 2⅞ in. (7.3 cm) squares

Construction

Half-square Triangles (page 22)
Flying Geese (page 24)
Four Patch (page 21)

Wide printed stripes can create a woven effect.

Seesaw

Size: 8 in. (20.3 cm) • **intermediate**

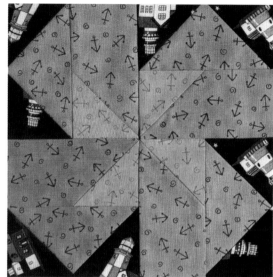

A

B

C

Cut the following

A Eight 4½ x 2½ in. (11.4 x 6.4 cm) strips
B Eight 2½ in. (6.4 cm) squares
C Four 2½ in. (6.3 cm) squares

Construction

Flying Geese (page 24)
Strips (page 25)
Four Patch (page 21)

Mix and match

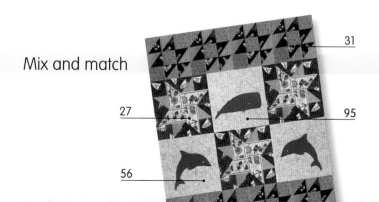

31
27
95
56

Mix and match

28
26
32

Four-patch Weave

Size: 12 in. (30.5 cm) • **easy**

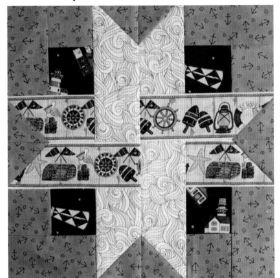

Cut the following

A Twelve 2½ in. (6.4 cm) squares
A Four 4½ x 2½ in. (11.4 x 6.4 cm) strips
B Four 2½ in. (6.4 cm) squares
C Two 4½ x 2½ in. (11.4 x 6.4 cm) strips
C Two 6½ x 2½ in. (16.5 x 6.4 cm) strips
D Two 4½ x 2½ in. (11.4 x 6.4 cm) strips
D Two 6 1/2 x 2 1/2" (16.5 x 6.4cm) strips

Construction

Parallelograms (page 24)
Nine Patch (page 21)

Wide printed stripes can create a woven effect.

Double X

Size: 6 in. (15.2 cm) • **intermediate**

Cut the following

A Three 2⅞ in. (7.3 cm) squares
B Three 2⅞ in. (7.3 cm) squares
C Two 2⅞ in. (7.3 cm) squares
D Two 2⅞ in. (7.3 cm) squares

Construction

Half-square Triangles (page 22)
Nine Patch (page 21)

Cut each square in half diagonally before arranging the pieces and sewing triangle squares.

Mix and match

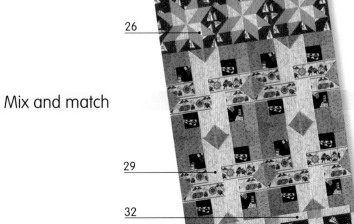

26

29

32

Mix and match

30

3

31 Jacks on Six

Size: 6 in. (15.2 cm) • **intermediate**

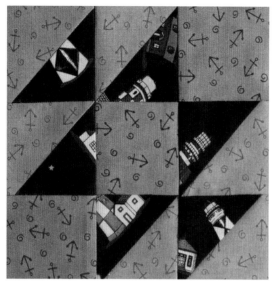

Construction

Half-square Triangles
(page 22)
Nine Patch (page 21)

Cut the following

A Three 2½ in. (6.4 cm) squares
B Three 2⅞ in. (7.3 cm) squares
C Three 2⅞ in. (7.3 cm) squares

32 Counterpane

Size: 6 in. (15.2 cm) • **easy**

Construction

Nine Patch (page 21)

Cut the following

A Four 4½ x 2½ in. (11.4 x
6.4 cm) strips
B One 4½ in. (11.4 cm) square
C Two 1½ in. (3.8 cm) squares
D Two 1½ in. (3.8 cm) squares

Mix and match

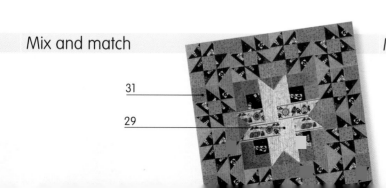

31

29

Mix and match

27

32

26

Northwind

Size: 6 in. (15.2 cm) • **intermediate**

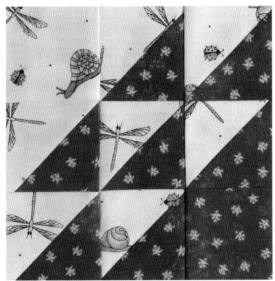

A

B

Cut the following

A One 2½ in. (6.4 cm) square
A Four 2⅞ in. (7.3 cm) squares
B One 2½ in. (6.4 cm) square
B Four 2⅞ in. (7.3 cm) squares

Construction

Half-square Triangles (page 22)
Nine Patch (page 21)

Birds in Flight

Size: 6 in. (15.2 cm) • **intermediate**

A

B

C

Cut the following

A Three 2½ in. (6.4 cm) squares
A Two 2⅞ in. (7.3 cm) squares
B Four 2⅞ in. (7.3 cm) squares
C Two 2⅞ in. (7.3 cm) squares

Construction

Half-square Triangles (page 22)
Nine Patch (page 21)

Cut each 2⅞ in. (7.3 cm) square
in half diagonally before
arranging the pieces and sewing
the triangle squares. Arrange the
stripes to create a woven effect.

Mix and match

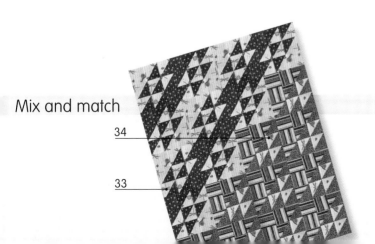

34

33

Mix and match

24

34

35

Cotton Reel

Size: 4 in. (10.2 cm) • **easy**

Construction

Half-square Triangles (page 22)
Four Patch (page 21)

Cut the following

A Two 2½ in. (6.4 cm) squares
B One 2⅞ in. (7.3 cm) square
C One 2⅞ in. (7.3 cm) square

Mix and match

35
88
28
26

Noah's Ark

Size: 12 in. (30.5 cm) • **intermediate**

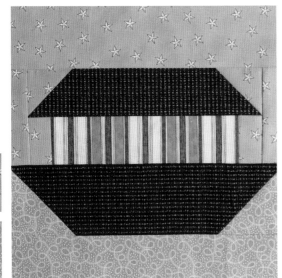

Construction

Flying Geese (page 24)
Strips (page 25)

Cut the following

A One 2½ x 3½ in. (6.4 x 8.9 cm) strip
A Two 4½ x 1½ in. (11.4 x 3.8 cm) strips
A Two 2½ x 1½ in. (6.4 x 3.8 cm) strips
A Two 2½ in. (6.4 cm) squares
B One 12½ x 2½ in. (31.8 x 6.4 cm) strip
B Two 3½ in. (8.9 cm) squares
C One 10½ x 2½ in. (26.7 x 6.4 cm) strip
C One 12½ x 3½ in. (31.8 x 8.9 cm) strip
D One 8½ x 2½ in. (21.6 x 6.4 cm) strip

Album Star

Size: 8 in. (20.3 cm) • **intermediate**

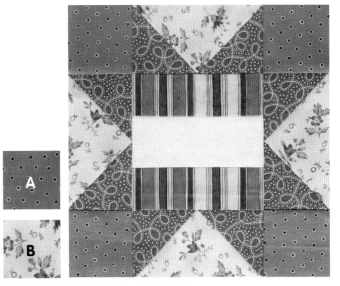

Construction

Flying Geese (page 24)
Nine Patch (page 21)

Write a name or a special
message on the plain
strip with an acid-free
permanent marker.

Cut the following

A Four 2½ in. (6.4 cm) squares
B Four 4½ x 2½ in. (11.4 x 6.4 cm)
strips
C Eight 2½ in. (6.4 cm) squares
D Two 4½ x 1¾ in. (11.4 x 4.4 cm)
strips
E One 4½ x 2 in. (11.4 x 5 cm) strip

Mix and match

66
79
99
80
36
109
20

60
98
61
59
14
105
70
85

Mix and match

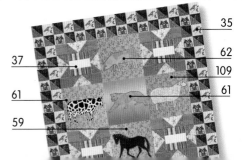

37
61
59

35
62
109
61

38 Nine Patch Fairy

Size: 6 in. (15.2 cm) • **easy**

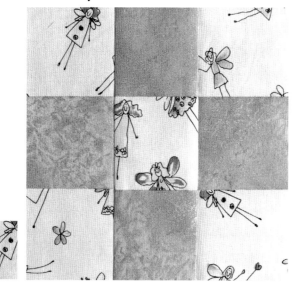

Construction

Nine Patch (page 21)

Cut the following

A Five 2½ in. (6.4 cm) squares
B Four 2½ in. (6.4 cm) squares

39 Abstract Flower

Size: 8 in. (20.3 cm) • **advanced**

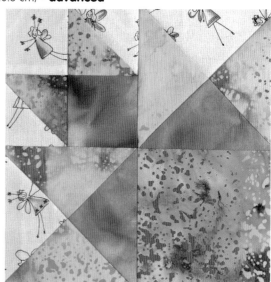

Construction

Half-square Triangles (page 22)
Four Patch (page 21)

Two quarters of B and C 5¼ in. (13.3 cm) squares will not be used so keep for another block.

Cut the following

A One 4½ in. (11.4 cm) square
A One 5¼ in. (13.3 cm) square, quartered diagonally
A One 2⅞ in. (7.3 cm) square, halved diagonally
B One 2½ in. (6.4 cm) square
B One 2⅞ in. (7.3 cm) square, halved diagonally
B & C One 5¼ in. (13.3 cm) square, quartered diagonally
C One 2½ in. (6.4 cm) square

Mix and match

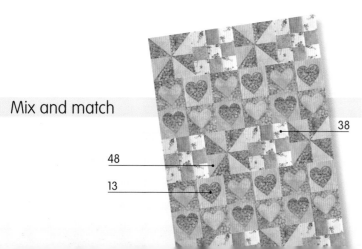

38
48
13

Mix and match

113
39

Four Patch

Size: 4 in. (10.2 cm) • **easy**

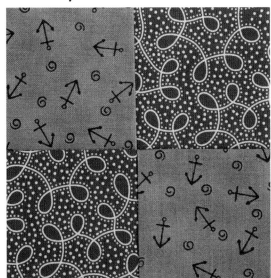

Construction

Four Patch (page 21)

Cut the following

A Two 2½ in. (6.4 cm) squares
B Two 2½ in. (6.4 cm) squares

Yellow Star

Size: 8 in. (20.3 cm) • **intermediate**

Construction

Flying Geese (page 24)
Nine Patch (page 21)

For the same color background throughout, cut A and D from pieces of the same fabric. For another variation, cut the center square and star points from the same fabric.

Cut the following

A Four 4½ in. (11.4 cm) squares
B Eight 2½ in. (6.4 cm) squares
C One 4½ in. (11.4 cm) square
D Four 4½ x 2½ in. (11.4 cm x 6.4 cm) strips

Mix and match

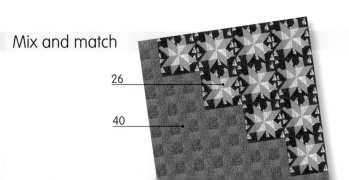

26

40

Mix and match

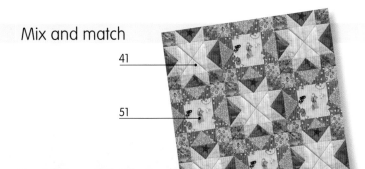

41

51

Tumbling Blocks

Size: 8 in. (20.3 cm) • **advanced**

A

B

C

D

Cut the following

A One 8½ in. (21.6 cm) square
B Three diamonds (page 116)
C Three diamonds (page 116)
D Three diamonds (page 116)

Construction

Make the patchwork using the English paper piecing method on page 26 and the templates on page 116. Remove the papers. Tuck all raw edges under the patchwork. Pin the patchwork to the 8½ in. (21.6 cm) backing square. Sew around the appliqué with machine blanket stitch or similar.

Grandmother's Flower Garden

Size: 8 in. (20.3 cm) • **advanced**

A

B

C

Cut the following

A One 2½ in. (6.4 cm) square
B Six hexagons (page 116)
C One hexagon (page 116)

Construction

Make the patchwork using the English paper piecing method on page 26 and the templates on page 116. Remove the papers. Tuck all raw edges under the patchwork. Pin the patchwork to the 8½ in. (21.6 cm) backing square. Sew around the appliqué with machine blanket stitch or similar.

Mix and match

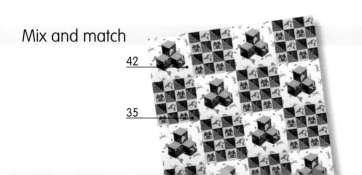

42

35

Mix and match

43

37

Hexagonal Flower and Pot

Size: 8 in. (20.3 cm) • **advanced**

Cut the following

A Ten 2½ in. (6.4 cm) squares
B Six hexagons (page 116)
C One hexagon (page 116)
D One flowerpot appliqué (page 119)
E One leaf appliqué (page 119)
Bonding material to back the flowerpot and leaf appliqués

Construction

Make the flowerpot and leaf appliqués using the templates on page 119. Follow the appliqué instructions on page 27. Iron on the appliqués to the 8½ in. (21.6 cm) square. Make the patchwork using the English paper piecing method on page 26 and the templates on page 116. Remove the papers. Tuck all raw edges under the patchwork. Pin the patchwork to the 8½ in. (21.6 cm) backing square. Sew around all the appliqués with machine blanket stitch or similar.

Hexagonal Flower Duo

Size: 12 in. (30.5 cm) • **advanced**

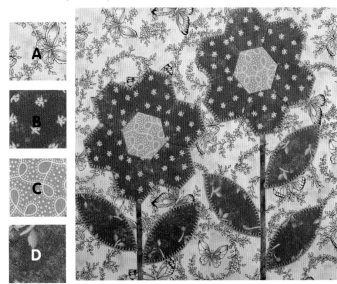

Cut the following

A One 12½ in. (31.8 cm) square
B Twelve hexagons (page 116)
C Two hexagons (page 116)
D Five leaf appliqués (page 119)
One 4 in. (10.2 cm) iron-on bias tape
One 6½ in. (16.5 cm) iron-on bias tape
Bonding material to back the leaf appliqués

Construction

Iron on the bias tape strips and sew in place. Make the leaf appliqués using the template on page 119. Follow the appliqué instructions on page 27. Iron on the leaf appliqués to the 12½ in. (31.8 cm) square. Make and appliqué the flowers as for block 43.

Mix and match

43
44
78

Mix and match

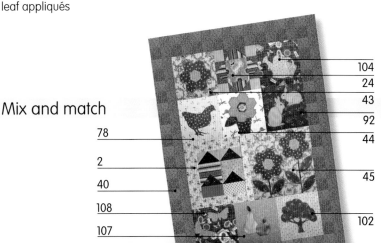

104
24
43
92
44
78
2
45
40
108
107
102

Grandmother's Favorite Variation

Size: 8 in. (20.3 cm) • **intermediate**

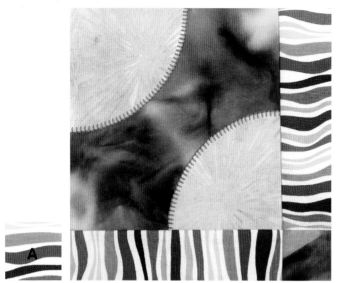

Cut the following

A Two 6½ x 2½ in. (16.5 x 6.4 cm) strips
B One 6½ in. (16.5 cm) diameter semicircle, halved
C One 6½ in. (16.5 cm) square
Bonding material to back the circle segment appliqués

Construction

Four Patch (page 21)

Following the appliqué instructions on page 27, iron the appliqué circle segments onto the 6½ in. (16.5 cm) square. Sew around the appliqué with machine blanket stitch or similar.

Maple Leaf

Size: 6 in. (15.2 cm) • **intermediate**

Cut the following

A Three 2½ in. (6.4 cm) squares
A Two 2⅞ in. (7.3 cm) squares
B Two 2½ in. (6.4 cm) squares
B Two 2⅞ in. (7.3 cm) squares
One 3 in. (7.6 cm) piece of green bias tape

Construction

Half-square Triangles (page 22)
Nine Patch (page 21)

Appliqué the bias tape to one 2½ in. (6.4 cm) square of fabric A.

Mix and match

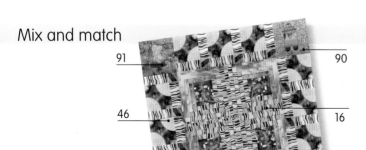

91
90
46
16

Mix and match

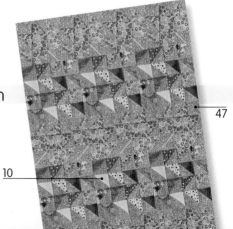

47
10

Pinwheel

Size: 6 in. (15.2 cm) • **intermediate**

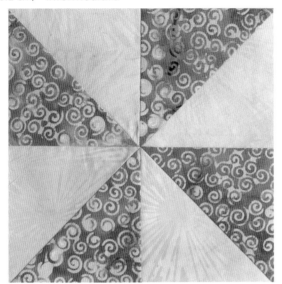

A

B

Cut the following

A Two 3⅞ in. (9.5 cm) squares
B Two 3⅞ in. (9.5 cm) squares

Construction

Half-square Triangles (page 22)
Four Patch (page 21)

Square in a Square II

Size: 4 in. (10.2 cm) • **easy**

A

B

Cut the following

A Four 2½ in. (6.4 cm) squares
B Two 1½ x 2½ in. (3.8 x 6.4 cm) strips
B Two 1½ x 4½ in. (3.8 x 11.4 cm) strips

Construction

Borders (page 25)

Mix and match

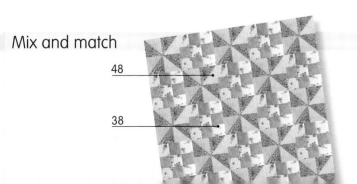

48

38

Mix and match

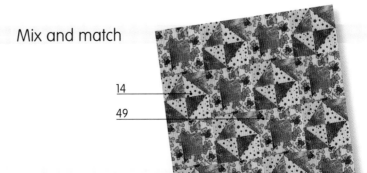

14

49

Antique Tile Variation

Size: 12 in. (30.5 cm) • *easy*

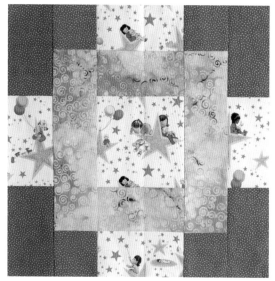

Cut the following

A Four 4½ x 2½ in. (11.4 x 6.4 cm) strips
A Four 2½ in. (6.4 cm) squares
B Four 4½ x 2½ in. (11.4 x 6.4 cm) strips
B One 4½ in. (6.4 cm) square
C Two 4½ x 2½ in. (11.4 x 6.4 cm) strips
C Two 8½ x 2½ in. (21.6 x 6.4 cm) strips

Construction

Strips (page 25)
Borders (page 25)

Eight-point Star

Size: 8 in. (20.3 cm) • *intermediate*

Cut the following

A Four 4½ in. (11.4 cm) squares
B Four 4½ x 2½ in. (11.4 x 6.4 cm) strips
C Eight 2½ in. (6.4 cm) squares
D One 4½ in. (11.4 cm) square

Construction

Flying Geese (page 24)
Nine Patch (page 21)

For a three-fabric version, use the same fabric for A and B or try a two-fabric version by using the same fabric for D and C.

Mix and match

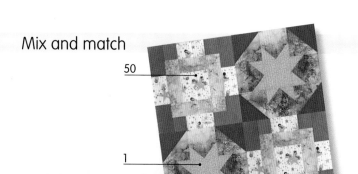

50

1

Mix and match

51

65

Beach Huts

Size: 8 in. (20.3 cm) • **intermediate**

Cut the following

A Two 4½ x 1½ in. (11.4 x 3.8 cm) strips
A One 4½ x 1½ in. (11.4 x 3.8 cm) strips
B Two 4½ x 1½ in. (11.4 x 3.8 cm) strips
C Two 4½ x 2½ in. (11.4 x 6.4 cm) strips
D One 4½ x 2½ in. (11.4 x 6.4 cm) strip
E One 8½ x 1½ in. (21.6 x 3.8 cm) strip
F One 8½ x 1½ in. (21.6 x 3.8 cm) strip
G Four 2½ in. (6.4 cm) squares

Construction

Flying Geese
(page 24)
Strips (page 25)

Mix and match

30
52

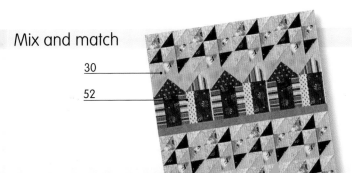

Appliqué

Appliqué is a lovely technique for making picture blocks for children's quilts. Most of the examples here require an intermediate skilll level, but beginners may want to start with the tractor (block 77) if they are new to the technique. Part of the joy of appliqué lies in selecting appropriate fabrics, such as the spotted textile used in the toadstool (block 68), or stripy textile used for the tiger (block 70).

Curious Cat

Size: 8 in. (20.3 cm) • **intermediate**

Cut the following

A One 8½ in. (21.6 cm) square
B One curious cat appliqué (page 114)
Bonding material to back the cat appliqué

Construction

Make the cat appliqué using the template on page 114. Follow the appliqué instructions on page 27. Iron on the appliqué to the 8½ in (21.6 cm) square. Sew around the appliqué with machine straight stitch or similar. Embroider the cat's face.

Mix and match

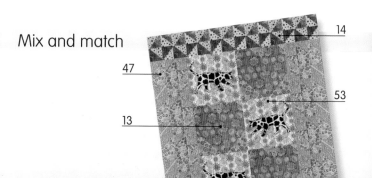

Sitting Cat

Size: 8 inches (20.3 cm) • **intermediate**

A

B

Cut the following

A One 8½ in. (21.6 cm) square
B One sitting cat appliqué
(page 113)
Bonding material to back the cat
appliqué

Construction

Make the cat appliqué
using the template on page
113. Follow the appliqué
instructions on page 27.
Iron the appliqué onto the
8½ in. (21.6 cm) square.
Sew around the appliqué
with machine straight stitch
or similar.

Cow

Size: 8 in. (20.3 cm) • **intermediate**

A

B

Cut the following

A One 8½ in. (21.6cm) square
B One cow appliqué (page 112)
Bonding material to back the
cow appliqué

Construction

Make the cow appliqué
using the template on page
112. Follow the appliqué
instructions on page 27.
Iron the appliqué onto the
8½ in. (21.6 cm) square. Sew
around the appliqué with
machine straight stitch or
similar. Embroider the
cow's face.

Mix and match

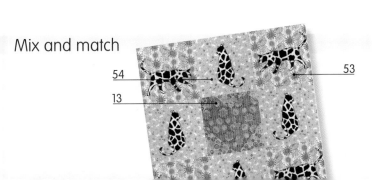

54
53
13

Mix and match

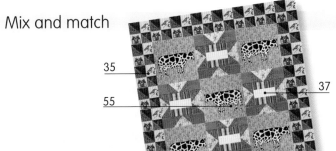

35
37
55

56 Dolphin

Size: 8 in. (20.3 cm) • **intermediate**

A

B

Cut the following

A One 8½ in. (21.6cm) square
B One dolphin appliqué
(page 111)
Bonding material to back the
dolphin appliqué

Construction

Make the dolphin appliqué
using the template on page
111. Follow the appliqué
instructions on page 27. Iron
on the appliqué to the 8½ in.
(21.6 cm) square. Sew around
the appliqué with machine
straight stitch or similar.
Embroider the dolphin's face.

57 White Duck

Size: 8 in. (20.3 cm) • **intermediate**

A

B

Cut the following

A One 8½ in. (21.6 cm) square
B One duck appliqué (page 113)
Bonding material to back the
duck appliqué

Construction

Make the duck appliqué
using the template on page
113. Follow the appliqué
instructions on page 27.
Iron on the appliqué to the
8½ in. (21.6 cm) square.
Sew around the appliqué
with machine straight
stitch or similar. Embroider
the duck's face.

Mix and match

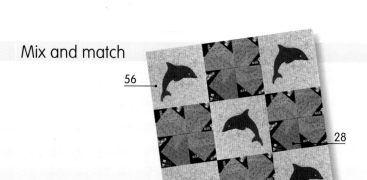

56

28

Mix and match

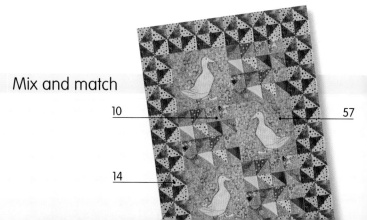

10

57

14

Hippo

Size: 8 in. (20.3 cm) • **intermediate**

A

B

Cut the following

A One 8½ in. (21.6 cm) square
B One hippo appliqué (page 111)
Bonding material to back the
hippo appliqué

Construction

Make the hippo appliqué
using the template on
page 111. Follow the
appliqué instructions on
page 27. Iron on
the appliqué to the
8½ in. (21.6 cm) square.
Sew around the appliqué
with machine straight
stitch or similar. Embroider
the hippo's face.

Horse

Size: 8 in. (20.3 cm) • **intermediate**

A

B

Cut the following

A One 8½ in. (21.6 cm) square
B One horse appliqué (page 114)
Bonding material to back the
horse appliqué

Construction

Make the horse appliqué
using the template on page
114. Follow the appliqué
instructions on page 27. Iron
on the appliqué to the 8½ in.
(21.6cm) square. Sew around
the appliqué with machine
straight stitch or similar.
Embroider the horse's face.

Mix and match

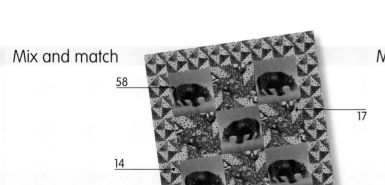

58
17
14

Mix and match

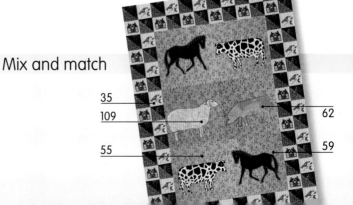

35
109
55
62
59

Lion

Size: 8 in. (20.3 cm) • **intermediate**

A

B

Cut the following

A One 8½ in. (21.6 cm) square
B One lion appliqué (page 119)
Bonding material to back the
lion appliqué

Construction

Make the lion appliqué using
the template on page 119. Follow
the appliqué instructions on
page 27. Iron on the appliqué
to the 8½ in. (21.6 cm) square.
Sew around the appliqué with
machine straight stitch or similar.
Embroider the lion's face.

Lioness

Size: 8 in. (20.3 cm) • **intermediate**

A

B

Cut the following

A One 8½ in. (21.6 cm) square
B One lioness appliqué (page 119)
Bonding material to back the
lioness appliqué

Construction

Make the lioness appliqué
using the template on page
119. Follow the appliqué
instructions on page 27.
Iron on the appliqué to the
8½ in. (21.6 cm) square.
Sew around the appliqué
with machine straight
stitch or similar. Embroider
the lioness's face.

Mix and match

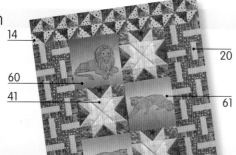

14
20
60
41
61

Mix and match

14
23
60
61

Pig

Size: 8 in. (20.3 cm) • **intermediate**

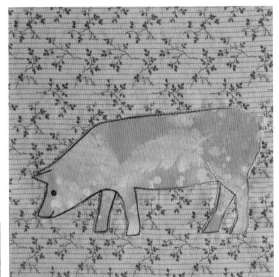

Cut the following

A One 8½ in. (21.6 cm) square
B One pig appliqué (page 115)
Bonding material to back the
pig appliqué

Construction

Make the pig appliqué using the
template on page 115. Follow
the appliqué instructions on
page 27. Iron on the appliqué
to the 8½ in. (21.6 cm) square.
Sew around the appliqué with
machine straight stitch or similar.
Embroider the pig's face.

Polar Bear

Size: 8 in. (20.3 cm) • **intermediate**

Cut the following

A One 8½ in. (21.6 cm) square
B One polar bear appliqué
(page 112)
Bonding material to back the
polar bear appliqué

Construction

Make the polar bear appliqué
using the template on page 112.
Follow the appliqué instructions
on page 27. Iron on the appliqué
to the 8½ in. (21.6 cm) square.
Sew around the appliqué with
machine straight stitch or similar.
Embroider the polar bear's face.

Mix and match

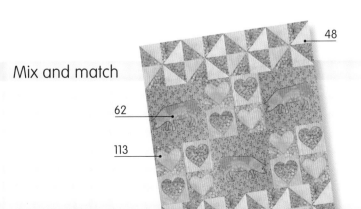

48

62

113

Mix and match

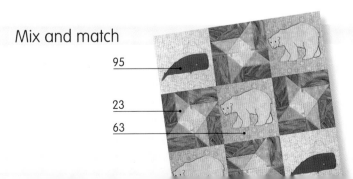

95

23

63

64 Smiling Sun

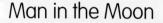

Size: 8 in. (20.3 cm) • **intermediate**

A

B

Cut the following

A One 8½ in. (21.6 cm) square
B One sun appliqué (page 116)
Bonding material to back the sun appliqué

Construction

Make the sun appliqué using the template on page 116. Follow the appliqué instructions on page 27. Iron on the appliqué to the 8½ in. (21.6 cm) square. Sew around the appliqué with machine satin stitch or similar. Embroider the sun's face.

Mix and match

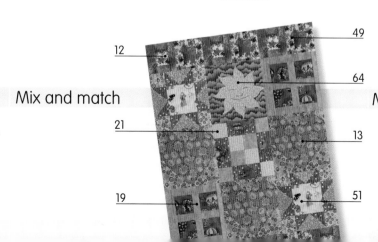

12
49
64
21
13
19
51

65 Man in the Moon

Size: 8 in. (20.3 cm) • **intermediate**

A

B

Cut the following

A One 8½ in. (21.6 cm) square
B One moon appliqué (page 116)
C One nightcap and tassel (page 116)
Bonding material to back the moon appliqué

Construction

Make the moon face, nightcap, and tassel appliqués using the template on page 116. Follow the appliqué instructions on page 27. Iron on the moon appliqué to the 8½ in. (21.6 cm) square. Position the nightcap appliqué and iron on, adding the tassel. Sew around the appliqué with machine satin stitch or similar. Embroider the moon's face.

Mix and match

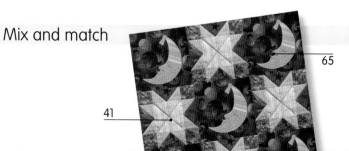

65
41

Camel

Size: 8 in. (20.3 cm) • **intermediate**

Cut the following

A One 8½ in. (21.6 cm) square
B One camel appliqué (page 114)
Bonding material to back the
camel appliqué

Construction

Make the camel appliqué
using the template on page
114. Follow the appliqué
instructions on page 27.
Iron on the appliqué to the
8½ in. (21.6 cm) square. Sew
around the appliqué with
machine straight stitch or
similar. Embroider the
camel's face.

Mix and match

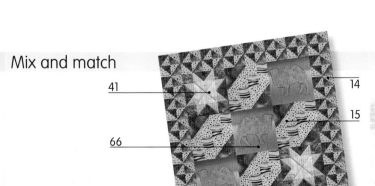

41
66
14
15

Fish

Size: 6 in. (15.2 cm) • **intermediate**

A

B

Cut the following

A One 6½ in. (16.5 cm) square
B Three fish appliqués (page 109)
Bonding material to back the
fish appliqués

Construction

Make the fish appliqués
using the template on page
109. Follow the appliqué
instructions on page 27. Iron
on the appliqués to the 6½ in.
(16.5 cm) square. Sew around
the appliqués with machine
straight stitch or similar.
Embroider the faces of the fish.

Toadstool

Size: 6 in. (15.2 cm) • **intermediate**

A

B

C

Cut the following

A One 6½ in. (16.5 cm) square
B One toadstool cap (page 109)
C One toadstool stalk
(page 109)
Bonding material to back
the toadstool cap and stalk
appliqués

Construction

Make the toadstool cap and stalk
appliqués using the template on
page 109. Follow the appliqué
instructions on page 27. Iron
on the appliqués to the 6½ in.
(16.5 cm) square, overlapping the
stalk and cap. Sew around the
appliqués with machine straight
stitch or similar.

Mix and match

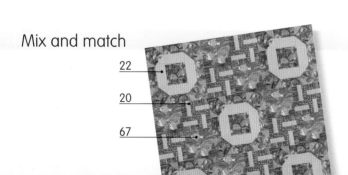

22

20

67

Mix and match

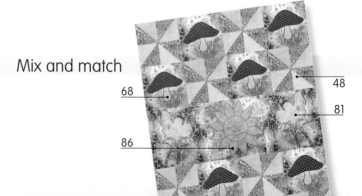

68

48

81

86

Airplane

Size: 8 in. (20.3 cm) • **intermediate**

Cut the following

A One 8½ in. (21.6 cm) square
B One airplane appliqué
(page 109)
Bonding material to back the
airplane appliqué

Construction

Make the airplane appliqué
using the template on page
109. Follow the appliqué
instructions on page 27.
Iron on the appliqué to
the 8½ in. (21.6 cm) square.
Sew around the appliqué
with machine straight stitch
or similar, adding the
detail lines as shown on
the template.

Tiger

Size: 8 in. (20.3 cm) • **intermediate**

Cut the following

A One 8½ in. square (21.6 cm)
B One tiger appliqué (page 120)
Bonding material to back the
tiger appliqué

Construction

Make the tiger appliqué using
the template on page 120. Follow
the appliqué instructions on
page 27. Iron on the appliqué
to the 8 ½ in. (21.6 cm) square.
Sew around the appliqué with
machine straight stitch or similar.
Embroider the tiger's face.

Mix and match

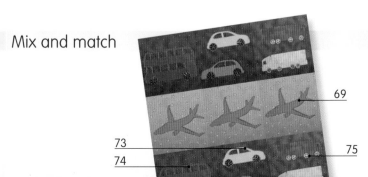

69
73
74
75

Mix and match

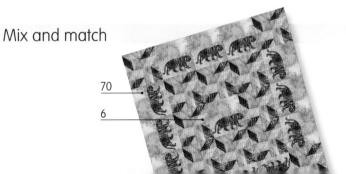

70
6

71 Balloon

Size: 8 inches (20.3cm) • **advanced**

A

B   C

Cut the following

A One 8½ in. (21.6 cm) square
B One balloon appliqué (page 118)
C One basket appliqué (page 118)
Bonding material to back the balloon appliqué

Construction

Make the balloon and basket appliqués using the templates on page 118. Follow the appliqué instructions on page 27. Iron on the appliqués to the 8½ in. (21.6 cm) square. Draw the lines linking the balloon and the basket. Sew around the appliqués with machine straight stitch or similar, adding the detail lines as shown on the template.

72 Brown Bear

Size: 8 in. (20.3 cm) • **intermediate**

A

B

Cut the following

A One 8½ in. (21.6 cm) square
B One bear appliqué
(page 117)
Bonding material to back the bear appliqué

Construction

Make the bear appliqué using the template on page 117. Follow the appliqué instructions on page 27. Iron on the appliqué to the 8½ in. (21.6 cm) square. Sew around the appliqué with machine straight stitch or a similar stitch, adding the detail lines as shown on the template. Embroider the bear's face.

Mix and match

20
21

19

71

Mix and match

72

82

Cars

Size: 8 in. (20.3 cm) • **intermediate**

Cut the following

A One 8½ in. (21.6 cm) square
B One green car appliqué (page 109)
C One orange car appliqué (page 109)
D Four wheel appliqués (page 109)
Bonding material to back the car appliqués

Construction

Make the car appliqués using the template on page 109. Follow the appliqué instructions on page 27. Make one car as a mirror image of the other. Iron on the appliqués to the 8½ in. (21.6 cm) square, overlapping the chassis and wheels. Sew around the appliqués with machine straight stitch or similar.

London Bus

Size: 8 in. (20.3 cm) • **intermediate**

Cut the following

A One 8½ in. (21.6 cm) square
B One bus appliqué (page 108)
C Two wheel appliqués (page 108)
Bonding material to back the bus appliqué

Construction

Make the bus appliqué using the template on page 108. Follow the appliqué instructions on page 27. Iron on the appliqué to the 8½ in. (21.6 cm) square, overlapping the bus and wheels. Sew around the appliqué with machine straight stitch or similar.

Mix and match

73   40   77   74

Mix and match

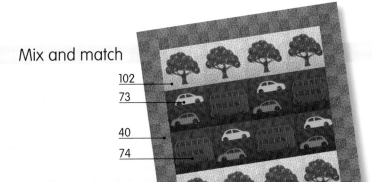

102   73   40   74

Trucks

Size: 8 in. (20.3 cm) • **intermediate**

Cut the following

A One 8½ in. (21.6 cm) square
B One red truck appliqué
(page 107)
C One yellow truck appliqué
(page 107)
D Eight wheel appliqués
(page 107)
Bonding material to back the
truck appliqués

Construction

Make the truck appliqués using
the template on page 107. Follow
the appliqué instructions on page
27. Make one truck as a mirror
image of the other. Iron on
the appliqués to the 8½ in.
(21.6 cm) square, overlapping the
chassis and wheels. Sew around
the appliqués with machine
straight stitch or similar.

Steam Train

Size: 8 in. (20.3 cm) • **intermediate**

Cut the following

A One 8½ in. (21.6 cm) square
B One train appliqué (page 109)
C Two large wheel appliqués
(page 109)
C Two small wheel appliqués
(page 109)
Bonding material to back the
train appliqués

Construction

Make the train appliqué using
the template on page 109
and following the appliqué
instructions on page 27. Iron the
appliqué onto the 8½ in.
(21.6 cm) square, overlapping
the train with the wheels. Sew
around the appliqué with
machine straight stitch or a
similar stitch.

Mix and match

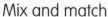

75
14

Mix and match

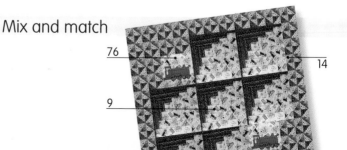

76
14
9

Tractor

Size: 8 in. (20.3 cm) • **easy**

A

B   **C**

Cut the following

A One 8½ in. (21.6 cm) square
B One tractor appliqué
(page 108)
C One large wheel appliqué
(page 108)
C One small wheel appliqué
(page 108)
Bonding material to back the
tractor appliqués

Construction

Make the tractor appliqué using
the template on page 108. Follow
the appliqué instructions on page
27. Iron on the appliqué to the 8½
in. (21.6 cm) square, overlapping
the chassis and the wheels. Sew
around the tractor with machine
straight stitch or similar. Sew
around the wheels with machine
blanket stitch or similar. Use
embroidery stitches to add tread
details to the wheels.

Chicken

Size: 8 in. (20.3 cm) • **intermediate**

A

B

Cut the following

A One 8½ in. (21.6 cm) square
B One chicken appliqué (page 120)
Bonding material to back the
chicken appliqué

Construction

Make the chicken appliqué
using the template on page
120. Follow the appliqué
instructions on page 27. Iron
on the appliqué to the 8½ in.
(21.6 cm) square. Sew around
the appliqué with machine
straight stitch or similar, adding
the detail lines as shown on
the template. Embroider the
chicken's face.

Mix and match

109
77
59
102
78

35
100
55
62

Mix and match

34
78

35

Dove of Peace

Size: 8 in. (20.3 cm) • **intermediate**

A

B

Cut the following

A One 8½ in. (21.6 cm) square
B One dove appliqué (page 109)
Bonding material to back the dove appliqué

Construction

Make the dove appliqué using the template on page 109. Follow the appliqué instructions on page 27. Iron on the appliqué to the 8½ in. (21.6 cm) square. Sew around the appliqués with machine straight stitch or similar, adding the detail lines as shown on the template. Add the leaf detail with green thread.

Mix and match

40

79

98

Elephant

Size: 8 in. (20.3 cm) • **intermediate**

Fairy Shadow

Size: 8 in. (20.3 cm) • **intermediate**

Cut the following

A One 8½ in. (21.6 cm) square
B One elephant appliqué (page 119)
Bonding material to back the elephant appliqué

Construction

Make the elephant appliqué using the template on page 119. Follow the appliqué instructions on page 27. Iron on the appliqué to the 8½ in. (21.6 cm) square. Sew around the appliqué with machine straight stitch or similar, adding the detail lines as shown on the template.

Cut the following

A One 8½ in. (21.6 cm) square
B One fairy appliqué (page 110)
Bonding material to back the fairy appliqué

Construction

Make the fairy appliqué using the template on page 110. Follow the appliqué instructions on page 27. Iron on the appliqué to the 8½ in. (21.6 cm) square. Sew around the appliqué with machine straight stitch or similar, adding the detail lines and fairy wand as shown on the template.

Mix and match

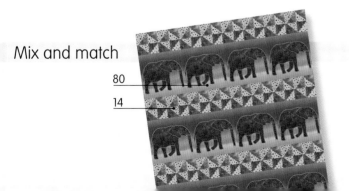

80
14

Mix and match

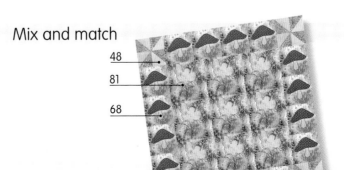

48
81
68

Fir Tree

Size: 8 in. (20.3 cm) • **intermediate**

A

B

Cut the following

A One 81/2 in. (21.6 cm) square
B One fir tree appliqué (page 115)
Bonding material to back the fir tree appliqué

Construction

Make the fir tree appliqué using the template on page 115. Follow the appliqué instructions on page 27. Iron on the appliqué to the 8½ in. (21.6 cm) square. Sew around the appliqué with machine straight stitch or similar.

Fox

Size: 8 in. (20.3 cm) • **intermediate**

A

B

Cut the following

A One 8½ in. (21.6 cm) square
B One fox appliqué (page 108)
Bonding material to back the fox appliqué

Construction

Make the fox appliqué using the template on page 108. Follow the appliqué instructions on page 27. Iron on the appliqué to the 8½ in. (21.6 cm) square. Sew around the appliqués with machine straight stitch or similar, adding the detail lines as shown on the template. Embroider the fox's face.

Mix and match

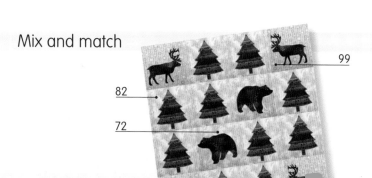

99
82
72

Mix and match

33
83
35

Frog

Size: 8 in. (20.3 cm) • **intermediate**

A

B

Cut the following

A One 8½ in. (21.6 cm) square
B One frog appliqué (page 117)
Bonding material to back the frog appliqué

Construction

Make the frog appliqué using the template on page 117. Follow the appliqué instructions on page 27. Iron the appliqué onto the 8½ in. (21.6 cm) square. Sew around the appliqués with machine straight stitch or similar, adding the detail lines as shown on the template. Embroider the frog's eyes.

Giraffe

Size: 8 in. (20.3 cm) • **intermediate**

A

B

Cut the following

A One 8½ in. (21.6 cm) square
B One giraffe appliqué (page 108)
Bonding material to back the giraffe appliqué

Construction

Make the giraffe appliqué using the template on page 108. Follow the appliqué instructions on page 27. Iron on the appliqué to the 8½ in. (21.6 cm) square. Sew around the appliqués with machine straight stitch or similar, adding the detail lines as shown on the template. Embroider the giraffe's face.

Mix and match

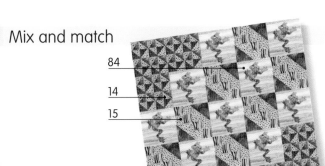

84
14
15

Mix and match

7
85
5
105

86 Happy Flower

Size: 8 in. (20.3 cm) • **intermediate**

A

B

Cut the following

A One 8½ in. (21.6 cm) square
B One flower appliqué (page 120)
Bonding material to back the flower appliqué

Construction

Make the flower appliqué using the template on page 120. Follow the appliqué instructions on page 27. Iron on the appliqué to the 8½ in. (21.6 cm) square. Sew around the appliqué with machine straight stitch or similar, adding the detail lines as shown on the template. Embroider the flower's face.

87 Lighthouse

Size: 8 in. (20.3cm) • **intermediate**

A

B

C

Cut the following

A One 8½ in. (21.6 cm) square
B One lighthouse appliqué (page 114)
B One lighthouse roof appliqué (page 114)
C One lamp room appliqué (page 114)
Bonding material to back the lighthouse appliqués

Construction

Make the lighthouse appliqué using the template on page 114. Follow the appliqué instructions on page 27. Iron on the appliqué to the 8½ in. (21.6 cm) square, overlapping the top and bottom of the lamp room appliqué with the other pieces. Sew around the appliqués with machine straight stitch, adding the detail lines as shown on the template.

Mix and match

38   68

81   86

Mix and match

40   8

56   87

26   27
                                      28

3

                                      95
                                      52

Little Footprints

Size: 8 in. (20.3 cm) • **intermediate**

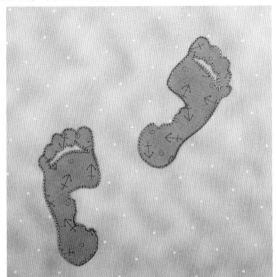

A

B

Cut the following

A One 8½ in. (21.6 cm) square
B Two footprint appliqués
(page 119)
Bonding material to back the
footprint appliqués

Construction

Make the footprint appliqués
using the template on page 119.
Follow the appliqué instructions
on page 27. Make one footprint
as a mirror image. Iron
on the appliqué to the
8½ in. (21.6 cm) square. Sew
around the appliqués
with machine straight stitch.

Little Handprints

Size: 8 in. (20.3 cm) • **intermediate**

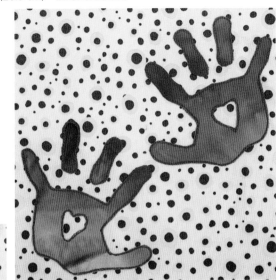

A

B

Cut the following

A One 8½ in. (21.6 cm) square
B Two handprint appliqués
(page 110)
Bonding material to back the
footprint appliqués

Construction

Make the handprint appliqués
using the template on page 110.
Follow the appliqué instructions
on page 27. Make one
handprint as a mirror image.
Iron on the appliqué to the
8½ in. (21.6 cm) square. Sew
around the appliqués
with machine straight stitch.

Mix and match

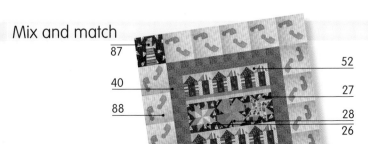

87
40
88
52
27
28
26

Mix and match

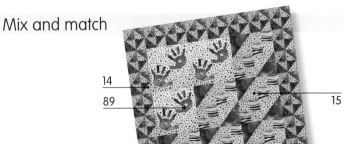

14
89
15

Overall Bill

Size: 8 in. (20.3 cm) • **intermediate**

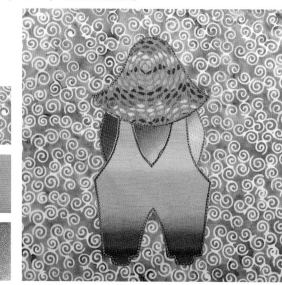

Cut the following

A One 8½ in. (21.6cm) square
B One overall appliqué (page 111)
C One shirt (circle) appliqué (page 111)
D One hat appliqué (page 111)
Bonding material to back all the appliqués

Construction

Make the Overall Bill appliqué using the templates on page 111. Follow the appliqué instructions on page 27. Iron on the appliqué to the 8½ in. (21.6 cm) square, overlapping the circle with the overalls, then the hat. Sew around the appliqués with machine straight stitch or similar.

Mix and match

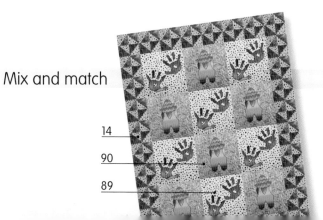

14
90
89

Sunbonnet Sue

Size: 8 in. (20.3 cm) • **intermediate**

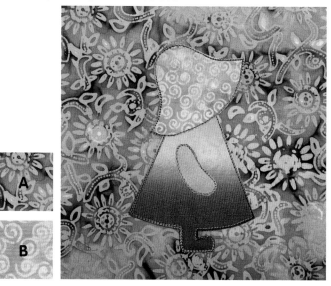

Cut the following

A One 8½ in. (21.6cm) square
B One hat appliqué (page 111)
C One dress appliqué (page 111)
D One arm appliqué (page 111)
Bonding material to back all the appliqués

Construction

Make the Sunbonnet Sue appliqué using the templates on page 111. Follow the appliqué instructions on page 27. Iron on the appliqué to the 8½ in. (21.6 cm) square, overlapping the dress with the arm, and the hat. Sew around the appliqués with machine straight stitch or a similar stitch.

Mix and match

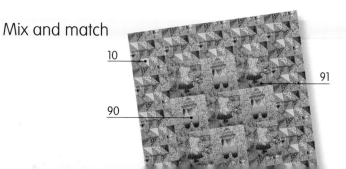

10
91
90

Rabbits

Size: 8 in. (20.3 cm) • **intermediate**

A

B

Cut the following

A One 8½ in. (21.6 cm) square
B One tall rabbit appliqué
(page 110)
B One small rabbit appliqué
(page 110)
Bonding material to back the
rabbit appliqués

Construction

Make the rabbit appliqués using
the templates on page 110.
Follow the appliqué instructions
on page 27. Iron on the
appliqués to the 8½ in.
(21.6 cm) square. Sew around
the appliqués with machine
straight stitch or similar, adding
the detail lines as shown on the
template. Embroider the faces of
the rabbits.

Penguins

Size: 8 in. (20.3 cm) • **intermediate**

A

B

C

Cut the following

A One 8½ in. (21.6 cm) square
B One penguin appliqué (page 107)
B One penguin profile appliqué
(page 107)
C Two penguin feet appliqué
(page 107)
C One penguin foot appliqué
(page 107)
C One penguin wing appliqué
(page 107)
C One penguin wing profile
appliqué (page 107)
Bonding material to back the
penguin appliqués

Construction

Make the penguin appliqués
using the templates on
page 107 and following the
appliqué instructions on
page 27. Cut fabric B pieces so
"wing" sections overlap slightly.
Iron the wing appliqués
to fabric B, then mark and
cut out penguins. Iron the
appliqués onto the 8½ in.
(21.6 cm) square, overlapping
the penguins' feet with their
bodies. Sew with straight stitch
and embroider the faces.

Mix and match

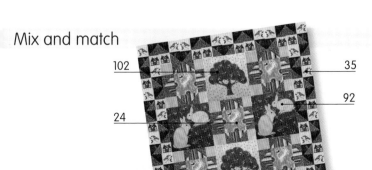

102   35

24   92

Mix and match

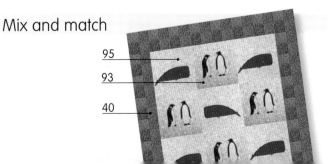

95

93

40

Chimpanzee

Size: 8 in. (20.3 cm) • **intermediate**

A

B

C

Cut the following

A One 8½ in. (21.6 cm) square
B One chimpanzee appliqué
(page 116)
C One chimpanzee face appliqué
Bonding material to back the
chimpanzee appliqué

Construction

Make the chimpanzee appliqué using the template on page 116. Follow the appliqué instructions on page 27. Iron the appliqué onto the 8½ in. (21.6 cm) square. Sew around the appliqué with machine straight stitch or similar. Iron on and embroider the chimpanzee's face.

Whale

Size: 8 in. (20.3 cm) • **intermediate**

A

B

Cut the following

A One 8½ in. (21.6 cm) square
B One whale appliqué
(page 116)
Bonding material to back the
whale appliqué

Construction

Make the whale appliqué using the template on page 116. Follow the appliqué instructions on page 27. Iron on the appliqué to the 8½ in. (21.6 cm) square. Sew around the appliqué with machine straight stitch or similar. Embroider the whale's face.

Mix and match

94
20
23
58

Mix and match

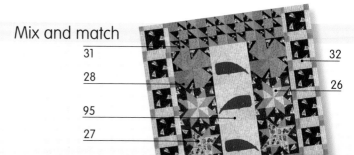

31
28
95
27
32
26

Dalmatian

Size: 8 in. (20.3 cm) • **intermediate**

Cut the following

A One 8½ in. (21.6 cm) square
B One dog appliqué (page 117)
Bonding material to back the
dog appliqué

Construction

Make the dog appliqué using the template on page 117. Follow the appliqué instructions on page 27. Iron on the appliqué to the 8½ in. (21.6 cm) square. Sew around the appliqué with machine straight stitch or similar, adding the detail lines as shown on the template. Embroider the dog's face.

Mix and match

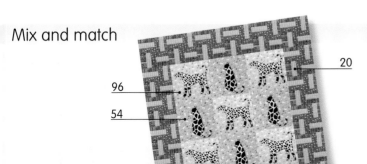

96
54
20

Rainbow Raindrops

Size: 8 in. (20.3 cm) • **intermediate**

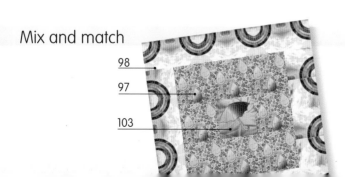

Cut the following

A One 8½ in. (21.6 cm) square
B Three raindrop appliqués
(page 111)
Bonding material to back the
raindrop appliqués

Construction

Make the raindrop appliqués
using the template on page 111.
Follow the appliqué instructions
on page 27. Iron on the
appliqués to the 8½ in.
(21.6 cm) square. Sew around the
appliqués with machine straight
stitch or similar. Embroider the
faces of the raindrops.

Mix and match

98
97
103

Rainbow

Size: 8 in. (20.3 cm) • **advanced**

Cut the following

A One 8½ in. (21.6 cm) square
B–F Rainbow appliqués
(page 118)
Bonding material to back the
rainbow appliqués

Construction

Make the rainbow appliqué
using the templates on page 118.
Follow the appliqué instructions
on page 27. Iron on the
appliqué to the 8½ in. (21.6 cm)
square, overlapping the curved
segments, beginning with the
largest segment. Sew along
the outer curves with machine
straight stitch or similar. For a
6 in. (15.2 cm) block, replace the
8½ in. (21.6 cm) square with a
6½ in. (16.5 cm) square.

Mix and match

110
98

Reindeer

Size: 8 in. (20.3 cm) • **advanced**

A

B

Cut the following

A One 8½ in. (21.6 cm) square
B One reindeer appliqué
(page 117)
Bonding material to back the
reindeer appliqué

Construction

Make the reindeer appliqué
using the template on page 117.
Follow the appliqué instructions
on page 27. Iron on the appliqué
to the 8½ in. (21.6 cm) square.
Sew around the appliqué with
machine straight stitch or similar,
taking care around the antlers.
Emboider the reindeer's face.

Rooster

Size: 8 in. (20.3 cm) • **intermediate**

A

B

Cut the following

A One 8½ in. (21.6 cm) square
B One rooster appliqué (page 120)
Bonding material to back the
rooster appliqué

Construction

Make the rooster appliqué using
the template on page 120. Follow
the appliqué instructions on
page 27. Iron on the appliqué
to the 8½ in. (21.6 cm) square.
Sew around the appliqué with
machine straight stitch or similar,
adding the detail lines as shown
on the template.

Mix and match

40
82
99

Mix and match

78
24
40
100

Seal

Size: 8 in. (20.3 cm) • **intermediate**

A

B

Cut the following

A One 8½ in. (21.6 cm) square
B One seal appliqué (page 107)
Bonding material to back the
rooster appliqué

Construction

Make the seal appliqué using the
template on page 107. Follow the
appliqué instructions on page 27.
Iron on the appliqué to the
8½ in. (21.6 cm) square. Sew
around the appliqué with
machine straight stitch or similar,
adding the detail lines as shown
on the template.

Tree

Size: 8 in. (20.3 cm) • **intermediate**

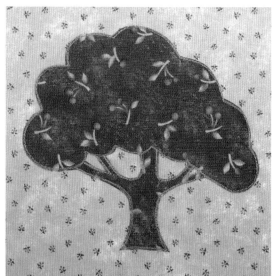

A

B

Cut the following

A One 8½ in. (21.6 cm)
square
B One tree appliqué
(page 118)
Bonding material to back
the tree appliqué

Construction

Make the tree appliqué using the
template on page 118. Follow the
appliqué instructions on page 27.
Iron on the appliqué to the 8½ in.
(21.6 cm) square. Sew around the
appliqué with machine straight stitch
or similar, adding the detail lines as
shown on the template.

Mix and match

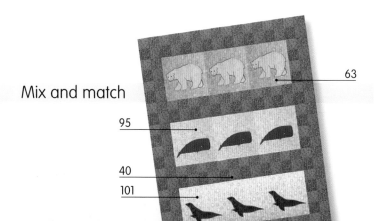

63

95

40

101

Mix and match

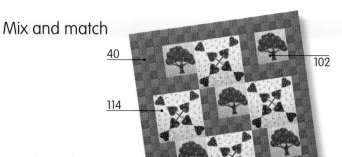

40

102

114

Umbrella

Size: 8 in. (20.3 cm) • **intermediate**

A

B

Cut the following

A One 8½ in. (21.6 cm) square
B One umbrella appliqué
(page 117)
Bonding material to back the
umbrella appliqué

Construction

Make the umbrella appliqué
using the template on
page 117. Follow the appliqué
instructions on page 27. Iron
on the appliqué to the 8½ in.
(21.6 cm) square. Sew around
the appliqué with machine
straight stitch or similar, adding
the detail lines as shown on
the template.

Watering Can

Size: 8 in. (20.3 cm) • **intermediate**

A

B

Cut the following

A One 8½ in. (21.6 cm) square
B One watering can appliqué
(page 118)
Bonding material to back the
watering can appliqué

Construction

Make the watering can appliqué
using the template on page 118.
Follow the appliqué instructions
on page 27. Iron on the appliqué
to the 8½ in. (21.6 cm) square.
Sew around the appliqué with
machine straight stitch or similar,
adding detail lines as shown on
the template.

Mix and match

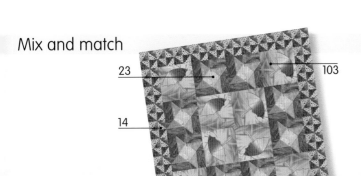

23
103
14

Mix and match

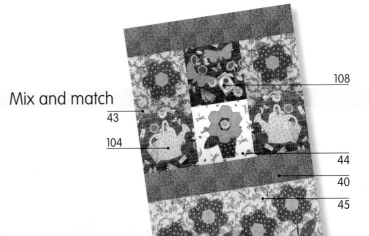

108
43
104
44
40
45

Zebra

Size: 8 in. (20.3 cm) • **intermediate**

Cut the following

A One 8½ in. (21.6 cm) square
B One zebra appliqué (page 112)
Bonding material to back the
zebra appliqué

Construction

Make the zebra appliqué
using the template on
page 112. Follow the
appliqué instructions
on page 27. Iron on the
appliqué to the 8½ in.
(21.6 cm) square. Sew
around the appliqué with
machine straight
stitch or similar. Embroider
the zebra's face.

Yellow Duck

Size: 8 in. (20.3 cm) • **intermediate**

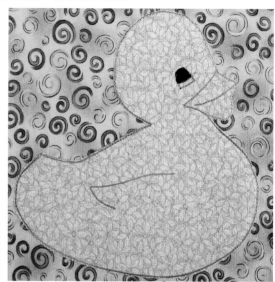

Cut the following

A One 8½ in. (21.6 cm) square
B One yellow duck appliqué
(page 110)
Bonding material to back the
yellow duck appliqué

Construction

Make the yellow duck appliqué
using the template on page 110.
Follow the appliqué instructions
on page 27. Iron on the
appliqué to the 8½ in.
(21.6 cm) square. Sew around
the appliqué with machine
straight stitch or similar, adding
the detail lines as shown on
the template. Embroider the
duck's eye.

Mix and match

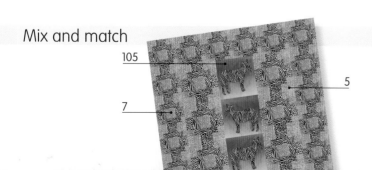

105

7

5

Mix and match

12

106

12

112

Apple and Pear

Size: 8 in. (20.3 cm) • **intermediate**

Cut the following

A One 8½ in. (21.6 cm) square
B One pear appliqué (page 115)
C One apple appliqué (page 115)
D Two leaf appliqués (page 115)
Bonding material to back the apple, pear, and leaf appliqués

Construction

Make the apple and pear appliqués using the templates on page 115. Follow the appliqué instructions on page 27. Iron on the appliqués to the 8½ in. (21.6 cm) square, overlapping the pear and apple. Add the leaves. Sew around the appliqués with machine straight stitch or similar, adding the leaf veins by sewing a line of stitches up the center of the leaf.

Butterflies

Size: 8 in. (20.3 cm) • **intermediate**

Cut the following

A One 8½ in. (21.6 cm) square
B two butterfly appliqués (page 120)
Bonding material to back the butterfly appliqués

Construction

Make the butterfly appliqués using the template on page 120 and following the appliqué instructions on page 27. Iron the appliqués onto the 8½ in (21.6 cm) square. Sew around the appliqués with machine straight stitch or similar, adding the butterflies' antennae, as shown.

Mix and match

107
35
102
40
21

Mix and match

44
108
43
104

Sheep

Size: 8 in. (20.3 cm) • **intermediate**

A

B

Cut the following

A One 8½ in. (21.6 cm) square
B One sheep appliqué (page 115)
Bonding material to back the
sheep appliqué

Construction

Make the sheep appliqué
using the template on page
115. Follow the appliqué
instructions on page 115.
Iron on the appliqué to the
8½ in. (21.6 cm) square.
Sew around the appliqué
with machine straight
stitch or similar. Embroider
the sheep's face.

Mix and match

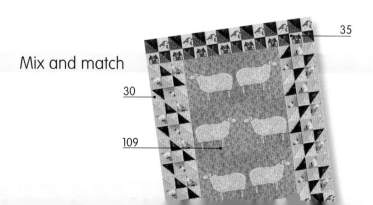

35
30
109

Cloud

Size: 8 in. (20.3 cm) • **intermediate**

A

B

Cut the following

A One 8½ in. (21.6 cm) square
B One cloud appliqué (page 116)
Bonding material to back the
cloud appliqué

Construction

Make the cloud appliqué
using the template on page
116. Follow the appliqué
instructions on page 27.
Iron on the appliqué to
the 8½ in. (21.6 cm) square.
Sew around the appliqué
with machine straight
stitch or similar. Embroider
the cloud's face.

Mix and match

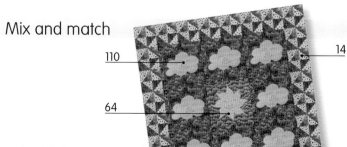

110
14
64

Dancing Teddy

Size: 8 in. (20.3 cm) • **intermediate**

A

B

Cut the following

A One 8½ in. (21.6 cm) square
B One dancing teddy appliqué
(page 113)
Bonding material to back the
teddy appliqué

Construction

Make the dancing
teddy appliqué using
the template on page
113. Follow the appliqué
instructions on page
27. Iron on the appliqué
to the 8½ in. (21.6 cm)
square. Sew around
the appliqué with
machine straight stitch
or similar. Embroider
the teddy's face.

Sitting Teddy

Size: 8 in. (20.3 cm) • **intermediate**

A

B

Cut the following

A One 8½ in. (21.6 cm) square
B One sitting teddy appliqué
(page 113)
Bonding material to back the
teddy appliqué

Construction

Make the sitting teddy
appliqué using the
template on page 113.
Follow the appliqué
instructions on page 27.
Iron on the appliqué to the
8½ in. (21.6 cm) square.
Sew around the appliqué
with machine straight stitch
or similar. Embroider the
teddy's face.

Mix and match

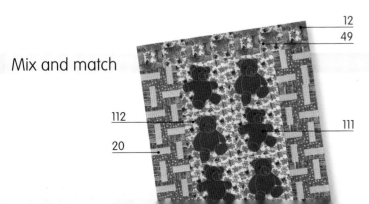

12
49
112
20
111

Mix and match

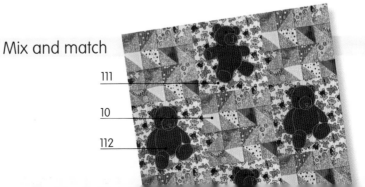

111
10
112

Four-patch Heart

Size: 8 in. (20.3 cm) • **intermediate**

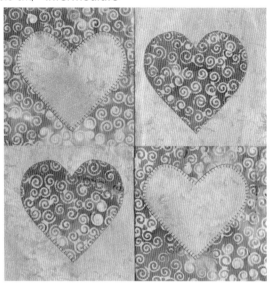

Cut the following

A Three 4½ in. (11.4 cm) squares
B Three 4½ in. (11.4 cm) squares
Two 4½ in. (11.4 cm) squares of bonding material

Construction

Four Patch (page 21)

Iron one 4½ in. (11.4 cm) square of bonding material to the back of one A and one B piece. Fold each one into quarters and cut out the hearts (see template, page 120). Iron one heart A to one square B. Repeat, alternating the fabrics. Sew around the hearts with machine satin stitch or similar.

Mix and match

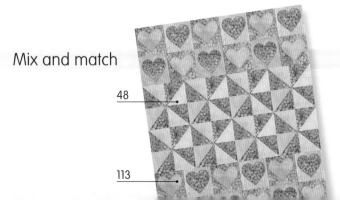

48

113

Hearts and Leaves

Size: 12 in. (30.5 cm) • **advanced**

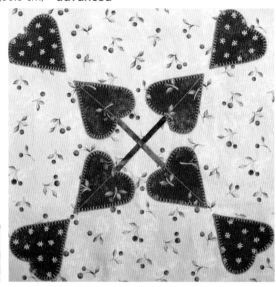

Cut the following

A Sixteen 2½ in. (6.4 cm) squares
B Four heart/leaf appliqués (page 120)
C Four heart/leaf appliqués (page 120)
Two 3½ in. (8.9 cm) pieces of iron-on bias tape
Bonding material to back the heart/leaf appliqués

Construction

Lightly mark diagonal lines through the center of the 12½ in. (31.8 cm) square to align the crossed bias tapes. Iron on the bias tape strips and sew them in place. Make the heart/leaf appliqués using the template on page 120. Follow the appliqué instructions on page 27. Iron on the leaf appliqués to the 12½ in. (31.8 cm) square. Sew around the appliqués with machine blanket stitch or similar.

Mix and match

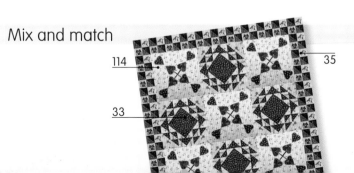

114

35

33

Letters and numbers

Use these alphabet and number appliqués in various ways. Spelling out baby's name and birth year with individual blocks is one idea. Add the letters to appliqué blocks for an illustrated alphabet, using a larger background square if necessary. You can use the numbers in the same way. For a special quilt, use the letters to write a message or sentiment around a plain border. Or go all the way with a full alphabet and numbers collection.

Alphabet "a"

Size: 6 inches (15.2 cm) • **intermediate**

A

B

Alphabet "b"

Size: 6 inches (15.2 cm) • **intermediate**

A

B

Alphabet "c"

Size: 6 inches (15.2 cm) • **intermediate**

A

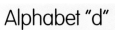B

Alphabet "e"

Size: 6 inches (15.2 cm) • **intermediate**

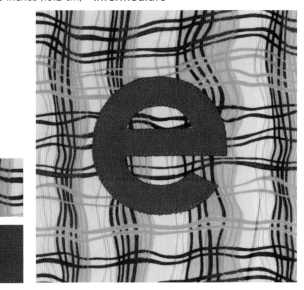

A

B

Alphabet "d"

Size: 6 inches (15.2 cm) • **intermediate**

A

B

Alphabet "f"

Size: 6 inches (15.2 cm) • **intermediate**

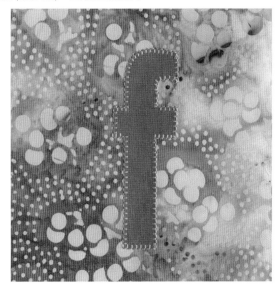

A

B

Alphabet "g"

Size: 6 inches (15.2 cm) • **intermediate**

A

B

Alphabet "i"

Size: 6 inches (15.2 cm) • **intermediate**

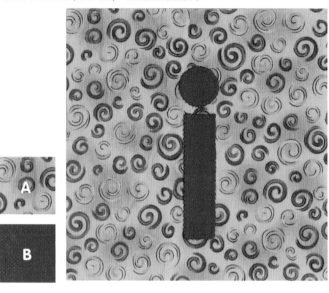

A

B

Alphabet "h"

Size: 6 inches (15.2 cm) • **intermediate**

A

B

Alphabet "j"

Size: 6 inches (15.2 cm) • **intermediate**

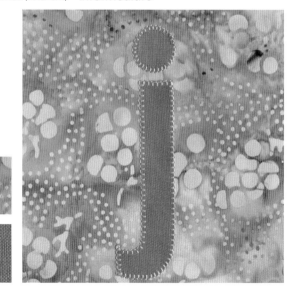

A

B

Alphabet "k"

Size: 6 inches (15.2 cm) • **easy**

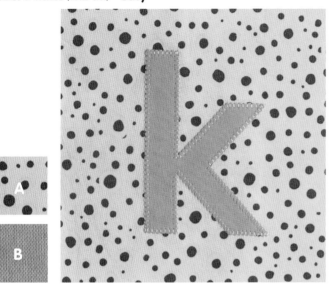

Alphabet "m"

Size: 6 inches (15.2 cm) • **intermediate**

Alphabet "l"

Size: 6 inches (15.2 cm) • **easy**

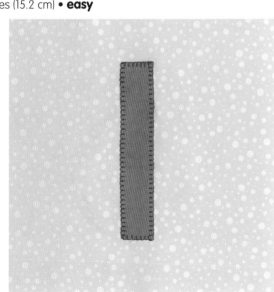

Alphabet "n"

Size: 6 inches (15.2 cm) • **intermediate**

Alphabet "o"

Size: 6 inches (15.2 cm) • **intermediate**

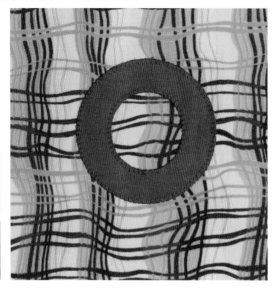

A

B

Alphabet "q"

Size: 6 inches (15.2 cm) • **intermediate**

A

B

Alphabet "p"

Size: 6 inches (15.2 cm) • **intermediate**

A

B

Alphabet "r"

Size: 6 inches (15.2 cm) • **intermediate**

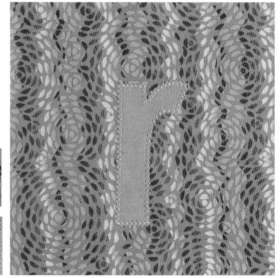

A

B

Alphabet "s"

Size: 6 inches (15.2 cm) • **easy**

Alphabet "u"

Size: 6 inches (15.2 cm) • **easy**

Alphabet "t"

Size: 6 inches (15.2 cm) • **easy**

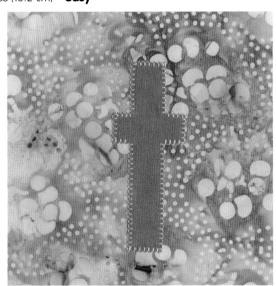

Alphabet "v"

Size: 6 inches (15.2 cm) • **easy**

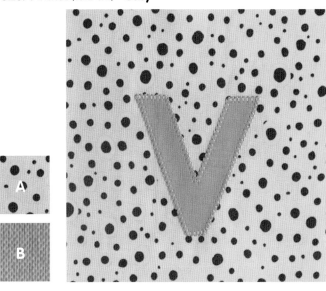

Alphabet "w"

Size: 6 inches (15.2 cm) • **easy**

Alphabet "y"

Size: 6 inches (15.2 cm) • **easy**

Alphabet "x"

Size: 6 inches (15.2 cm) • **easy**

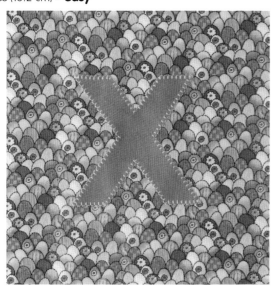

Alphabet "z"

Size: 6 inches (15.2 cm) • **easy**

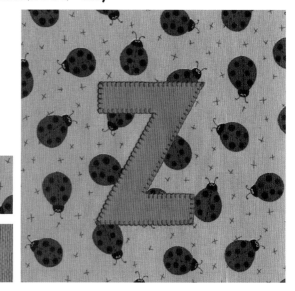

Number "0"

Size: 6 inches (15.2 cm) • **intermediate**

Number "1"

Size: 6 inches (15.2 cm) • **easy**

Number "2"

Size: 6 inches (15.2 cm) • **easy**

A

B

Number "4"

Size: 6 inches (15.2 cm) • **easy**

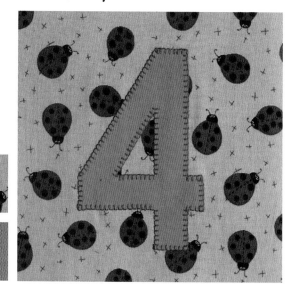

A

B

Number "3"

Size: 6 inches (15.2 cm) • **intermediate**

A

B

Number "5"

Size: 6 inches (15.2 cm) • **intermediate**

A

B

Number "6"

Size: 6 inches (15.2 cm) • **intermediate**

Number "8"

Size: 6 inches (15.2 cm) • **intermediate**

Number "7"

Size: 6 inches (15.2 cm) • **easy**

Number "9"

Size: 6 inches (15.2 cm) • **intermediate**

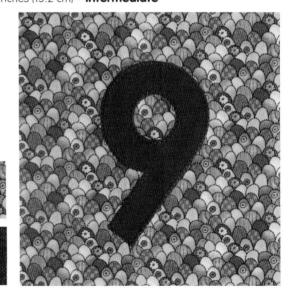

section three

Appliqué templates

This library of appliqué templates provides a rich resource of images that you can combine in different ways and use to personalize your quilts. You could also design your own templates—adapt simple outline drawings, coloring book illustrations, and favorite cartoon characters.

Making templates

The templates in this section can be used to make the appliqué blocks, or you can modify their arrangement in your own designs. You can flip templates and use them as mirror images. Experiment with color—you could have a brown cow or a blue spotty one! You can combine several templates on a larger block or appliqué to a long border or larger quilt center.

Preparing templates

Enlarge the templates by the percentage indicated using a photocopier or an "all in one" computer printer scanner; most have a percentage increase facility, just follow the instructions on the machine's display panel. Trace the designs so you can turn them over and use mirror images—some photocopiers enable you to flip the image directly from the page. Before you begin, check the details of each appliqué design, and note that some designs have several pieces.

Penguins
increase by 40%

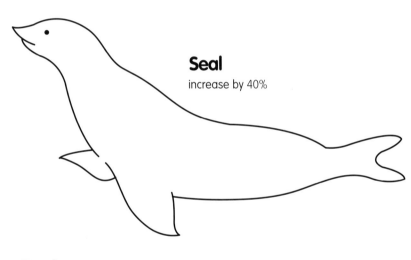

Seal
increase by 40%

Truck
increase by 40%

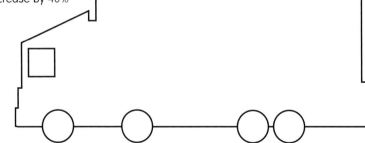

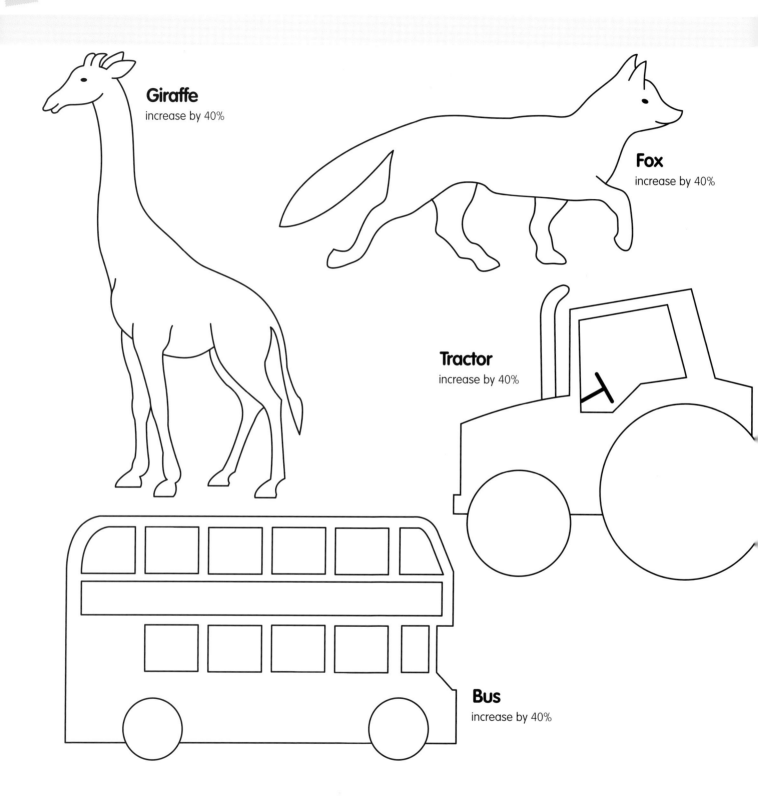

Giraffe
increase by 40%

Fox
increase by 40%

Tractor
increase by 40%

Bus
increase by 40%

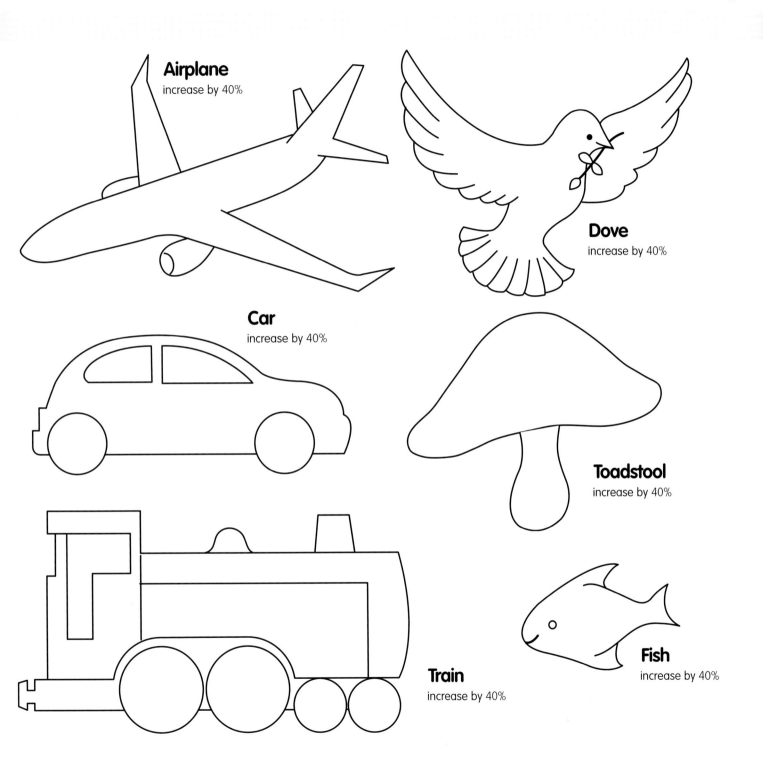

Airplane
increase by 40%

Dove
increase by 40%

Car
increase by 40%

Toadstool
increase by 40%

Train
increase by 40%

Fish
increase by 40%

Small Rabbit
increase by 40%

Tall Rabbit
increase by 40%

Fairy
increase by 40%

Yellow Duck
increase by 40%

Handprint
increase by 40%

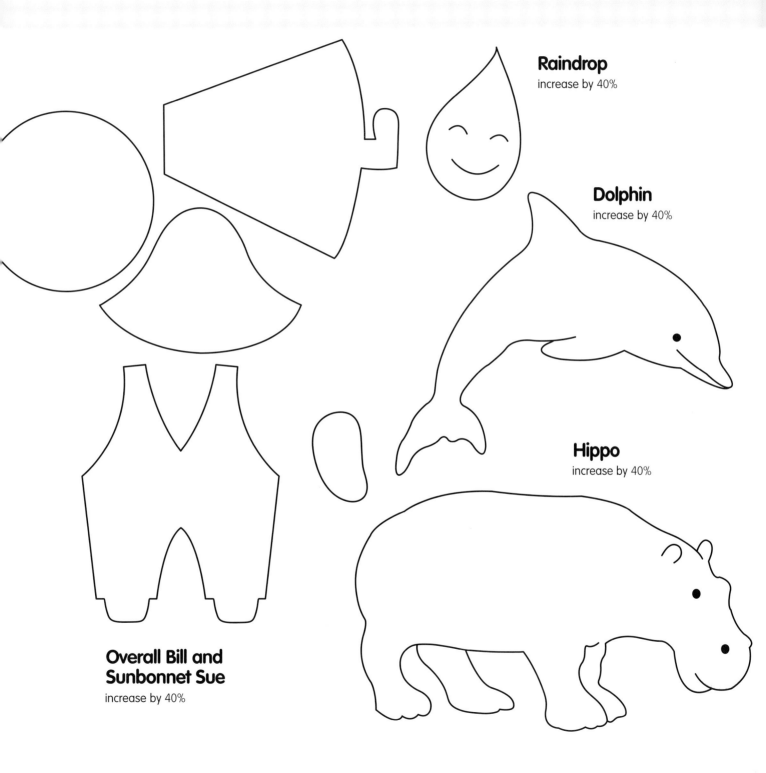

Raindrop
increase by 40%

Dolphin
increase by 40%

Hippo
increase by 40%

**Overall Bill and
Sunbonnet Sue**
increase by 40%

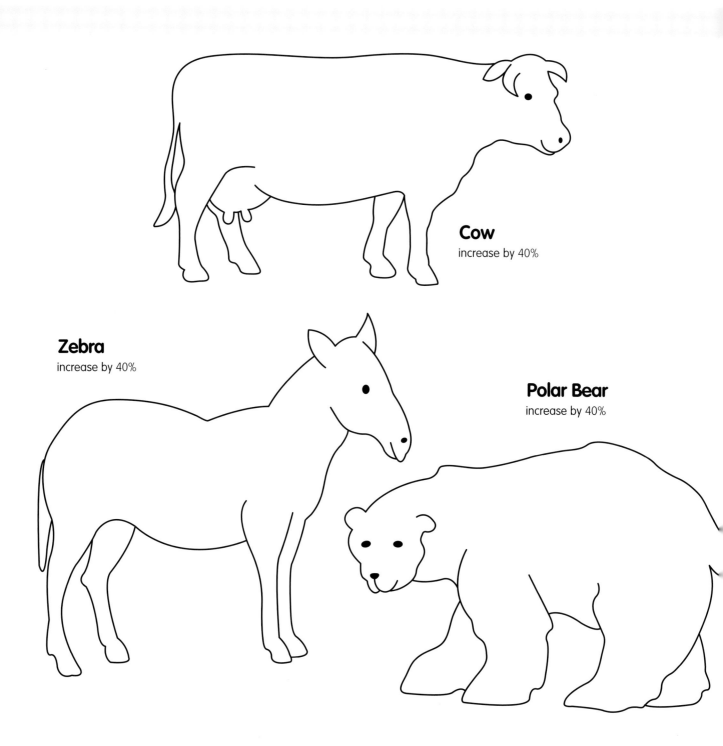

Cow
increase by 40%

Zebra
increase by 40%

Polar Bear
increase by 40%

Duck
increase by 40%

Sitting Teddy
increase by 40%

Dancing Teddy
increase by 40%

Sitting Cat
increase by 40%

Horse
increase by 40%

Curious Cat
increase by 40%

Camel
increase by 40%

Lighthouse
increase by 40%

Pig
increase by 40%

Leaf
increase by 40%

Apple
increase by 40%

Sheep
increase by 40%

Fir Tree
increase by 40%

Pear
increase by 40%

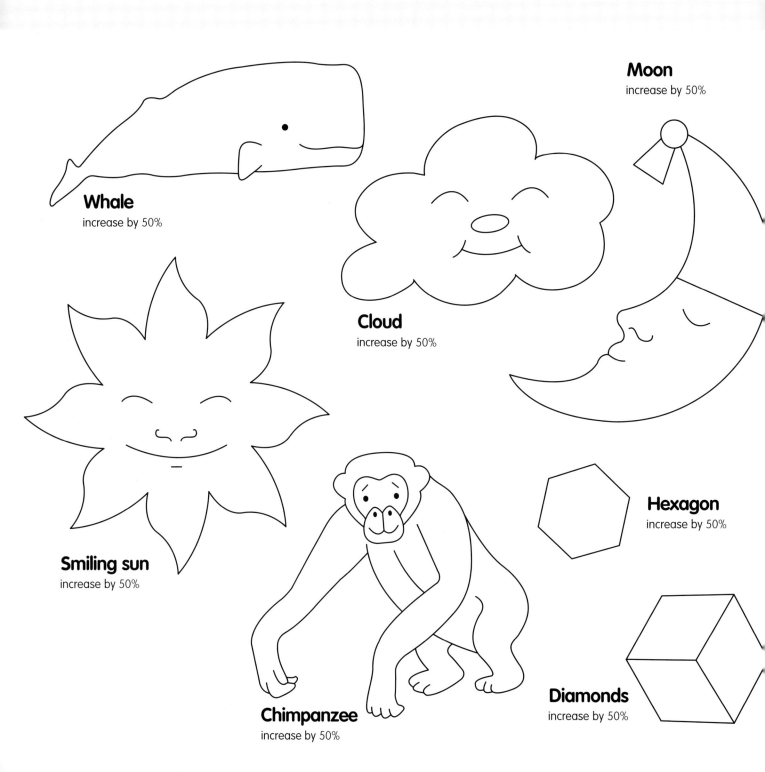

Whale
increase by 50%

Cloud
increase by 50%

Moon
increase by 50%

Smiling sun
increase by 50%

Chimpanzee
increase by 50%

Hexagon
increase by 50%

Diamonds
increase by 50%

Bear
increase by 50%

Frog
increase by 50%

Dog
increase by 50%

Reindeer
increase by 50%

Umbrella
increase by 50%

Balloon
increase by 50%

Tree
increase by 50%

Watering Can
increase by 50%

Rainbow
increase by 50%

Flowerpot
increase by 50%

leaf
increase by 50%

Lion
increase by 50%

Lioness
increase by 50%

Elephant
increase by 50%

Footprint
increase by 50%

Happy Flower
increase by 50%

Rooster
increase by 50%

Chicken
increase by 50%

Heart / Leaf
increase by 50%

Tiger
increase by 50%

Butterfly
increase by 50%

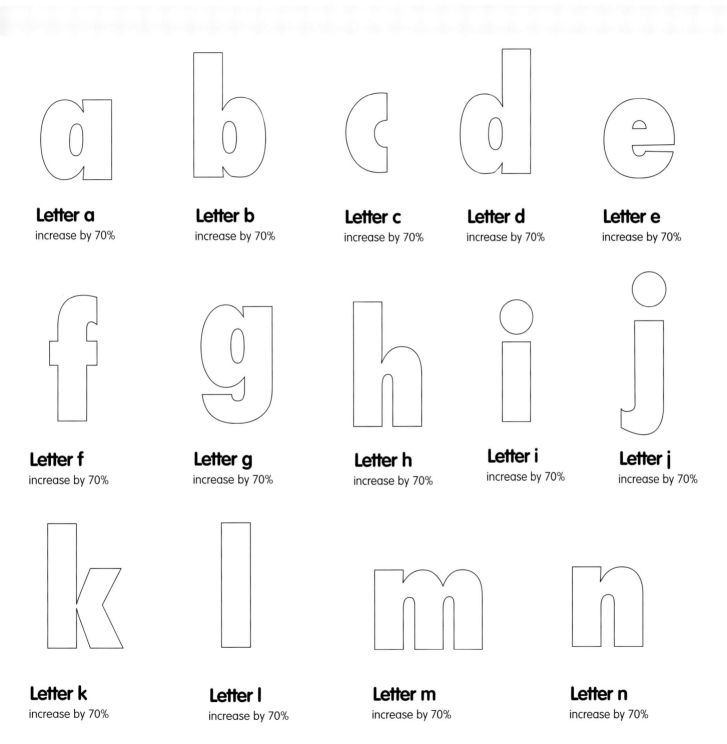

Letter a
increase by 70%

Letter b
increase by 70%

Letter c
increase by 70%

Letter d
increase by 70%

Letter e
increase by 70%

Letter f
increase by 70%

Letter g
increase by 70%

Letter h
increase by 70%

Letter i
increase by 70%

Letter j
increase by 70%

Letter k
increase by 70%

Letter l
increase by 70%

Letter m
increase by 70%

Letter n
increase by 70%

Letter o
increase by 70%

Letter p
increase by 70%

Letter q
increase by 70%

Letter r
increase by 70%

Letter s
increase by 70%

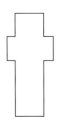

Letter t
increase by 70%

Letter u
increase by 70%

Letter v
increase by 70%

Letter w
increase by 70%

Letter x
increase by 60%

Letter y
increase by 60%

Letter z
increase by 60%

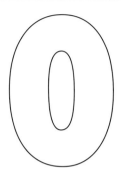

Number 0

increase by 60%

Number 1

increase by 60%

Number 2

increase by 60%

Number 3

increase by 60%

Number 4

increase by 60%

Number 5

increase to 60%

Number 6

increase by 60%

Number 7

increase by 60%

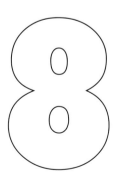

Number 8

increase by 60%

Number 9

increase by 60%

Index

Resources

Mail Order Suppliers

USA

eQuilter.com
5455 Spine Road
Suite E; Boulder
CO 80301 USA
Tel: USA Toll Free: 877-FABRIC-3
or: 303-527-0856
E-mail: service@equilter.com
www.eQuilter.com

Hancocks of Paducah
3841 Hinkleville Road
Paducah
KY
USA 42001
tel: USA Toll Free 1-800-845-8723
International 1-270-443-4410
E-mail: customerservice@hancocks-
paducah.com
www.hancocks-paducah.com

The City Quilter
133 West 25th Street
New York, NY 10001
tel: 212-807-0390
E-mail: info@cityquilter.com
www.cityquilter.com

UK

The Cotton Patch
1285 Stratford Road
Hall Green
Birmingham
B28 9AJ
tel: 0121 702 2840
E-mail: mailorder@cottonpatch.net
www.cottonpatch.co.uk

Hannah's Room
50 Church Street
Brierley
Barnsley
South Yorkshire
S72 9HT
tel: 01226 713427
E-mail: sales@hannahsroom.co.uk
www.hannahsroom.co.uk

Patchwork Corner
51 Belswains Lane
Hemel Hempstead
Hertfordshire
HP3 9PW
tel: 01442 259000
E-mail: jenny@patchworkcorner.co.uk
www.patchworkcorner.com

Credits

While every effort has been made to credit contributors, Quarto would like to apologize should there have been any omissions or errors, and would be pleased to make the appropriate correction for future editions of the book.

Quarto would also like to thank our models Isabelle Crawford and Ava Bergeaud-Marko.